House Rules
10 Guidelines *for* Christian Homes

House Rules

10 Guidelines *for* Christian Homes

JACOB HUDGINS

House Rules: 10 Guidelines for Christian Homes

Copyright © 2023 by Jacob Hudgins. All Rights Reserved.

All rights reserved. No part of this book may be reproduced in any form or by any electronic or mechanical means including information storage and retrieval systems, without permission in writing from the author. The only exception is by a reviewer, who may quote short excerpts in a review.

Interior designed by Project Go

Visit my website at www.jacobhudgins.com

Printed in the United States of America

ISBN 978-1-7352970-3-3

To Team Hudgins: Sarah, Luke, Noah, and Josie.

Thanks for letting me be a family with you.

The Rules

1 Home is a safe place.

2 All people deserve respect.

3 We tell the truth.

4 We speak with love.

5 No gossip allowed.

6 We take responsibility.

7 We deal with our problems.

8 We lead by serving.

9 We control ourselves.

10 Just because you're angry doesn't mean you're right.

Table *of* Contents

Introduction   1

RULE 1
Home Is a Safe Place   9

RULE 2
All People Deserve Respect   22

RULE 3
We Tell the Truth   37

RULE 4
We Speak with Love   51

RULE 5
No Gossip Allowed   63

RULE 6
We Take Responsibility   78

RULE 7
We Deal with Our Problems   94

RULE 8
We Lead by Serving   112

RULE 9
We Control Ourselves   125

RULE 10
Just Because You're Angry Doesn't Mean You're Right   141

Conclusion: Keep Sowing the Seeds!   157

Works Cited   161

Introduction

"What starts here changes the world." The University of Texas adopted this grandiose slogan for a series of TV advertisements in 2002. As a graduate of one of UT's bitterest rivals, I found it full of hubris. What starts *here*—and only *here*—changes the world? While I understand the goal—appealing to ambitious students who long to make a difference—it all sounds a bit much.

Assertions like these always sound overblown. How many people truly "change the world" or "make a difference"? And just how strongly can we correlate those differences with the school one chooses to attend?

Yet despite aversion to hyperbole, I can say this confidently: *What starts at home changes the world.*

WHY HOMES MATTER

Home is both a place and a concept. Throughout this book, I will use the term to refer to our close, regularly present family. In particular, home encompasses husband/wife relationships and parent/child relationships. These are the closest bonds we have. Home can be a place of tremendous comfort and nurture—or a source of violent rage and deep hurt. Often it is a blend of the two. *Home is where our deepest relationships are lived out. It is the place where kids' hearts are formed. Home is also the people who teach us the most important lessons and see us at our lowest points.* If we get home wrong, we cause unspeakable damage. If we get home right, we can change the world. The stakes could not be higher.

Homes are habit incubators.

My mother taught me to address adults as "sir" and "ma'am." In our home, we never said "yeah" to a grown-up. For years my mother interrupted my speech—or her own—to correct me about this. To this day I can still recall her asking me, "Sir?", which was my cue to remember to say "ma'am". And to this day, I cannot address anyone older than myself without "sir" or "ma'am." When traveling in the northeastern U.S., I spoke with an older lady I had just met. Unprompted, she asked, "You're from the south, aren't you?". I asked her how she guessed (fearing I was showing off a southern twang). "We don't say, 'ma'am' up here. We just say 'yeah.'" Thanks, Mom.

We are deeply formed by the habits we learn in the home. Some are habits of speaking—words we don't say and words we do. Some are idiosyncratic customs like eating dinner around the table, dividing up the chores, or holding the door for others. Some are much more important, such as whether we approve of alcohol (and how much), whether violence is allowed, or whether pornography is acceptable. Yet all of these habits are reinforced indelibly by the combination of physical proximity, emotional togetherness, and time that are unique to a home.

When a home is formed, a culture begins. We have our own rules and customs. If we come from another home, we travel with the baggage of past family cultures. I contend that *we must be intentional about allowing Christian thinking to saturate and form our family cultures*. We must let Jesus and the New Testament inform our habits.

Homes are growth engines.

It is astonishing to watch babies I held in my hands grow taller than me. Sometimes my wife and I shake our heads and ask each other, "How did this happen?". Growth is a natural phenomenon that consistently amazes us. Yet the internal maturity that happens at home may be more impressive. In a few short years, children move from speechlessness to expressing opinions about abstract concepts. They learn manners, develop tastes, and gain a moral compass. All of this takes place *somewhere*—and ideally, that somewhere is in the home.

Because of this—and the impressionability of youth—there is a biblical focus on the urgency of helping children grow now. "Discipline your son, for there is hope" (Prov 19:18). "Discipline your son, and he will give you rest; he will give delight to your heart" (Prov 29:17). "Train up a child in the way he should go; even when he is old he will not depart from it" (Prov 22:6). I have heard this principle illustrated in a variety of ways. Children are like trees: the way you bend them as saplings becomes the way they harden and stabilize. Children are like wet cement: the things you teach them in youth are permanently etched into their hearts and character. All of these proverbs and illustrations call our attention to the extreme importance of the home as a place where growth can be appropriately guided.

But homes are also growth engines for husbands and wives. Marriages changes us. In his extended meditation on the spiritual benefits of marriage, Gary Thomas argues, "Any situation that calls me to confront my selfishness has enormous spiritual value, and I slowly began to understand that the real purpose of marriage may not be happiness as much as it is holiness."[1] Even after a few weeks together, husbands and wives grow. Sometimes we grow more selfish,

---

1. Thomas, p. 22.

sometimes less. Sometimes closer together, sometimes farther apart. Sometimes more spiritual, sometimes less. As we orbit each other, we have an undeniable impact on each other's character and spiritual development. Homes matter because *they involve the people who will have the biggest impact on our growth of anyone on earth.*

Homes are hypocrisy revealers.

Christians often dress up for church. We wear our "Sunday best"—clothes that do not come out the rest of the week. Children are forced to shower and comb their hair. We arrive at church buildings looking and smelling our best. In short, at church, we appear to be entirely different people than we actually are.

This veneer can often involve more than our dress. We smile and nod and shake hands and compliment other Christians. We pay close attention to sermons and sing out. Yet as we drive away from worship, we bicker with our spouse, complain about what Brother Fussbudget said, and yell at the kids. Which version of ourselves is the *real* us?

Homes are hypocrisy revealers. Our families know what we *really* think, how we *really* feel, and what we *really* believe. They know when our faith is only skin-deep or is reserved for Sundays. They know when our actions don't match up with our talk. And they know when we truly, deeply, sincerely follow Jesus.

And our families are influenced by our own hypocrisy—or lack thereof. Children are watching to learn how what they are expected to do, say, and believe—and what that will actually mean in practice. So if, as a Christian father, I allow my anger to reign, I not only scar my family and cause them to live in fear of me, but I also lead my children to react in the same way. How can I discipline them for their lack of control when I have not disciplined myself? How can I quote the Bible to them when I don't follow it? In time, my mixed messages create a crisis for my family: Do they follow my talk, my actions, or neither?

If we can truly see the impact our walk with Jesus has on our families, we may be motivated to finally tackle the serious spiritual deficiencies in our own hearts.

Jean Vanier, founder of the l'Arche communities, speaks of community in this same way: "Community is the place where our limitations, our fears and our egoism are revealed to us. We discover our poverty and our weakness, our inability to get on with some people, our mental and emotional blocks, our affective or sexual disturbances, our seemingly insatiable desires, our frustrations and jealousies, our hatred and our wish to destroy."[2] Like a close-knit community, our homes reveal something significant about us. We cannot fake it. Our response to what we learn about ourselves at home becomes a tremendous test of character. What kinds of people will we prove to be among those who know us best?

Homes feed societies.

I often hear Christians express concern about the direction of American society. What is odd to me about these complaints is that they usually have a helpless tone. Well, our country is falling apart on us, but what can you do? Here is my answer: *we can build Christian homes!* Christian homes feed men and women of character and conviction into our society to become the salt and light of the next generation.

When we teach our children to control themselves, speak with love, and lead by serving, we do not only contribute to *their* well-being. We also place another vessel for God's use into our kids' schools. These attitudes and actions become a part of a learning environment, then a workplace. Churches begin to change. Neighborhoods reflect

---

2. Vanier, p. 26.

a new, Christ-centered perspective. Our cities look a little different. The contagious nature of the gospel perspective can renew our nation from the bottom up—and Christian homes are the key.

What starts at home changes the world.

DO WE REALLY NEED MORE RULES?

Marriage and parenting have proven far more challenging and far more rewarding than I expected. One of the most difficult parts of being a husband and father (of three) is that logistical concerns often push out spiritual needs. It is hard to plan formal family Bible studies when we are traveling to basketball games and Girl Scouts. The urgency of each day's schedule conflicts with our stated goal of spiritual instruction. Similar difficulties crop up in marriage, where we can grow too busy—or too concerned about rocking the boat—to truly address our spiritual weaknesses.

House rules are important because *we need a plan, reminders, and a sound direction*. What are the core values you will pursue in your home? What will matter most to you? When one child refuses to share with another child, will you emphasize the need for boundaries or the need for sacrifice? When your mate angers you but you don't want to fight, will you emphasize the need for peace or the need for honesty? All homes operate by rules; it is essential that we choose these rules according to Scripture.

I find it important to *name our values*. Giving the rules in our home a name means that we can come back to them again and again. They are virtues to pursue. Everyone must follow them, even Mom and Dad. They are eternally true and good. Stating values also means that everyone knows when someone has violated important rules. There is no question as to why it causes a problem. These are the rules of the house.

WHY THIS BOOK?

This book originated with me noticing a heartbreaking reality. Many Christians teach and believe lofty doctrines but have poor home lives. Their children are out of control—or completely checked out—or deeply bitter. Their marriages are of the "ships passing in the night" variety—or ones in which passing comments hint at profound bitterness. So many Christians seem miserable. Worse, they often seem to pour their disenchantment and anger into a harsh form of the Christian faith.

Yet I did not write this book to criticize such people. *I wrote it because I am terrified that I will become them.* I love my family dearly and I want to lead them like Jesus. I also love Jesus dearly and want that faith to go all the way into the core of my home. I am supremely confident that Jesus knows what he is talking about. If we can make Christian homes more Christian, the collateral blessings will be staggering.

As I thought about these things, I also had a job to do as husband and father. With a limited number of areas and lessons to focus on, the question quickly arises: Which principles are the most essential ones? In my role as a preacher, I needed to teach lessons on Christian living, including parenting. And the children in our congregation need to be taught, so our parents also need to be reminded. I began to collect what I determined to be the most important lessons for a Christian home. You may disagree about their importance (or think others should be added to the list), but I hope we can all agree that the rules in this book are biblical.

I grew up in a Christian home, but not a peaceful one. There is a unique type of heartache and struggle that children of troubled and broken homes know. I am desperate to avoid such a climate in my home. I would do anything in my power to save others from it. God's vision for the home is rich and inspiring: "Behold, children are a heritage from the LORD, the fruit of the womb a reward. Like arrows in the hand of a warrior are the children of one's youth. Blessed is the man who fills his quiver with them! He shall not be put to shame when he speaks with his enemies in the gate" (Psalm 127:3-5). God intends families to be a source of great joy. He wants our homes to be beautiful, peaceful, and fruitful.

My prayer is that by practicing these rules in your home, you will challenge yourself and lead your family closer to Jesus.

What starts at home changes the world. God is with us. Let's change the world!

RULE 1

Home is a Safe Place

What home should be is often far different from what home is.

The word "home" conjures a sense of belonging, warmth, and peace. Home is where we fit. Home is where we act like, think like, and (usually) look like the people around us. Home is where we share interests, visions, and clothes. Home is where we laugh and sometimes cry and always love.

But for many people, this is not home. For many, home is a place of contention and hostility, abuse and fear, pain and hate. For many, home is Dad stumbling home drunk and irrationally angry. For many, home is a miserable marriage to a perpetually fault-finding mate. For many, home is never-ending arguments and unreachable expectations. For many, home is a place where discussion and dissent are squashed.

For many people—both in our time and throughout history—home is *not* a safe place.

This does incalculable damage. Children grow up believing that there is nowhere where they are free to express their thoughts and feelings. No one loves them unconditionally. The most important people in their lives can never be pleased. Nowhere is safe. Spouses cower in fear, wary that honesty will lead to violence. Love gives way to annoyance—or irritation—or eventually despair.

Christian homes must be different. *Home is a safe place.*

We struggle with extremes in our perception about our homes. We think of a family as either lenient or strict, loving or disciplined. We make swift, far-flung judgments about others (Can you believe he said that to his wife? He's so controlling!). We make unwarranted, anxiety-ridden evaluations about our own homes (Will my son resent me when he is grown if I send him to his room?). Given these tendencies, we might overlook the fundamental value of safety, thinking that if we focus on it, we sacrifice the right to correct each other. This is a false dilemma. If our families are not safe at home, there is no way that we can pursue any of the other Christian values our homes will rest on. We can ensure safety without growing permissive, worldly, or anxious. God wants our homes to be safe, but never at the expense of proper Christian teaching.

If we love our families, they should feel safe with us. Children and spouses need physical, emotional, and spiritual safety. Home should be a haven from dangers. Homes can be places where we are free to grow, express ourselves, and learn to love—without fear.

THE SCRIPTURAL CALL TO SAFETY

Modern people often speak condescendingly about the home lives of ancient peoples. These were the times, we insist, when men were considered dictators, women property, and children seen and not heard. To be sure, there were severe deficiencies in Jewish and Greco-Roman homes. Yet this is what makes the scriptural call to safety so notable. Paul talked about home being a safe place long before it was cool.

> Fathers, do not provoke your children to anger, but bring them up in the discipline and instruction of the LORD (Eph 6:4).

> Fathers, do not provoke your children, lest they become discouraged (Col 3:21).

In their parenting, Paul cautions fathers that they can "provoke (their) children to anger" (Eph 6:4) or parent them in such a way that they become "discouraged" (Col 3:21). While each person is accountable for their own actions and responses, it is clear that parents can cause problematic reactions in their children. Paul does not want children to obey parents at just any cost. Some parenting strategies—or lack thereof—lead to embittered, discouraged children. Without compromising one bit on the need for teaching and correction, Paul calls on fathers to make home a safe space for their children.

At times safety can be confused with permissiveness. Paul is not telling parents that they cannot challenge a child about their behavior, speech, or attitude. Nor is he telling them that any parental guidance that angers or discourages is forbidden. He is stressing the need for safety.

When we parent our children so that they do not know what is allowed or forbidden, we frustrate them. When we discipline out of anger or embarrassment (rather than the well-being of our child), we dishearten them. When we are violent, they may cower in the short-term, but over time they grow defiant, deeply bitter, and perhaps even violent themselves. When they are not allowed to voice their thoughts and opinions, they resent us. The children will spend years working through their anger and discouragement, but Paul says that the parents are at fault. They have not made home safe.

> Husbands, love your wives, and do not be harsh with them (Col 3:19).

> Husbands, love your wives as Christ loved the church and gave himself up for her…In the same way husbands should love their wives as their own bodies. He who loves his wife loves himself. For no one ever hated his own flesh, but nourishes and cherishes it, just as Christ does the church (Eph 5:25, 28-29).

> Likewise, husbands, live with your wives in an understanding way, showing honor to the woman as the weaker vessel, since they are heirs with you of the grace of life, so that your prayers may not be hindered. (1 Pet 3:7)

Meanwhile, Paul also urges husbands to show tenderness to their wives. "Husbands, love your wives, and do not be harsh with them" (Col 3:19). Love is contrasted with harshness. Paul is not merely instructing Christian husbands to be chivalrous, polite, or occasionally gentlemanly. He is emphasizing that husbands must take the lead in maintaining a safe home. *Our wives should not fear us.* Harshness is utterly inappropriate. If Paul draws the line at harshness, then there is absolutely no room for threats, violence, or abuse. Home is a safe place.

As a model of the kind of tender love he is promoting, Paul points us to Jesus. "Love your wives as Christ loved the church and gave himself up for her" (Eph 5:25). The distinctive part of Jesus' love for his people is that *he never considers his own needs, but freely offers himself up for his beloved.* The model of the Christian husband is not demanding, discontent, or critical. He is self-giving, honoring his wife to the degree that there is no reasonable grounds to question his complete devotion.

Perhaps a comparison that is closer to home is that "husbands should love their wives as their own bodies" (Eph 5:28). We are carefully and constantly aware of the state of our bodies—particularly if some part is hurting. We do not usually treat ourselves roughly. "For no one ever hated his own flesh, but nourishes and cherishes it." Husbands should nourish and cherish our wives. The words here mean to feed and care for our bodies (and, therefore, our wives). This is more than protection or provision; it is nurture.

Peter also urges Christian husbands to "live with (their) wives in an understanding way" (1 Pet 3:7). The word "understanding" means "according to knowledge." One commentator argues that "here it is not analytical knowledge or religious insight that is intended, but personal insight that leads to loving and considerate care, whether in the bedroom or in other activities of marriage."[1] Christian husbands live with their wives in "loving and considerate care."

The wife is worthy of honor. Peter tells husbands to "(show) honor to the woman as the weaker vessel" (1 Pet 3:7). The "weaker vessel" is an odd and confusing phrase. While it could be that Peter is reflecting contemporary beliefs that women are the weaker sex, it seems more likely to me that he is challenging his culture by urging men to treat their wives gently. A weaker vessel is one that is delicate and fragile. It is not that women cannot handle the harshness of men; it is that *they shouldn't have to*. Christian husbands should understand the need for intentional care in the way we interact with our wives. We show them honor. We respect their value. We are careful with them—their bodies, their hearts, and their feelings. This is not because women are lesser, but because we esteem their *more highly*. We love them, so we refuse to mistreat them. They feel safe with us.

Peter adds a cautionary note to this instruction about how husbands treat their wives: "since they are heirs with you of the grace of life, so that your prayers may not be hindered" (1 Pet 3:7). He envisions a marriage of two believers and reminds husbands that *their wives are children of God too*. They are joint-heirs, without any whisper of different status before God. Marriages involve the joining of equals—and Peter stresses that husbands must continue to behave as if this is the case.

Husbands also honor their wives "so that your prayers may not be hindered." The implications here are staggering. God is watching over our homes to see how we treat our mates. If we are unkind and abusive to our mates—if we refuse to show them honor—if we neglect one another—our relationship with God is in jeopardy.

---

1. Davids, in loc.

Hindered prayers are the result of a fractured relationship with God. We often think that this can only come about because of scandalous sin or a complete rejection of the faith. Here Peter says the truth is much closer to home. A few verses later, Peter quotes from Psalm 34: "Whoever desires to love life and see good days, let him keep his tongue from evil and his lips from speaking deceit; let him turn away from evil and do good; let him seek peace and pursue it. For the eyes of the LORD are on the righteous, and his ears are open to their prayer. But the face of the LORD is against those who do evil" (1 Pet 3:10-12). The logic of the passage is simple: God answers the prayers of people committed to serving him. But Peter's application is shocking: God will not answer the prayers of those who do not treat their mates well. Making our homes safe has vital spiritual importance.

God is calling us to make our homes safe places.

SAFE TO SPEAK

Honesty is a high priority for Christians. "Therefore, having put away falsehood, let each one of you speak the truth with his neighbor, for we are members one of another" (Eph 4:25). When Jesus teaches on oaths, he prescribes a simple forthrightness in our speaking: "Let what you say be simply 'Yes' or 'No'; anything more than this comes from evil" (Matt 5:37). Our manner of speaking reflects our commitment to honesty.

Yet behind the priority of honesty is the assumption that we are free to speak. For honesty to have any meaning, we must have the opportunity to lie. For respect to have any meaning, there must be the potential for disrespect. We will not build character in our homes by terrifying our family members into proper speech. Our goal is to make an environment in which it is safe to speak—and then *convincing* one another to speak like Jesus wants us to.

Rule 1: Home is a Safe Place

Little Jane is 5 years old. She is beginning to be able to tell time and understand that she has to go to bed when the clock says 8:30. At some point it occurs to her that this is arbitrary, so she asks, "Dad, why do I have to go to bed at 8:30?" Dad responds by forcefully telling her, "Stop complaining and do what you're told!". Jane's question is not answered or even entertained. Jane learns that for some reason Dad gets angry about bedtimes, that she has done something wrong, and that it is not safe to speak in her house.

Tom is suspicious of his wife. She has been spending a lot of time away from him and he is confused and scared that she is seeing another man. Yet he remembers that the last time he asked her about her behavior, she raised her voice and accused *him*. He decides that it is not safe to talk with her about his concerns—and instead he should just try to catch her in the act.

Home is a place where *we should be safe to speak about our feelings and concerns*. Vanier says that "community is the safe place where all of us feel free to be ourselves and have the confidence to say everything we live and think."[2] Being safe to speak does not mean that children don't still have to learn respect. Some words will still anger other people. Safety does not guarantee agreement. We will still need discretion. Yet in a safe home, we are free to express ourselves, challenge others, and tell others how we feel.

Is everyone in the home free to say that they are upset or frustrated? Is there room to ask for clarification about a parental decision? Can husbands and wives frankly discuss an issue and know that they will be heard? Or is the home one in which one person brooks no dissent, hogs the spotlight, or shouts down all opposition?

Creating safety in this way is about our reactions. Do we respond with kindness and understanding when our spouses and children express themselves? Are we overly critical? Are we listening carefully? Sometimes what is said is not always what is meant; do we

---

2. Vanier, p. 53.

ask questions before reacting? Do we give the benefit of the doubt? What our family members say can still upset or disappoint us, but we must value safety to speak.

SAFE TO FAIL

None of us is perfect. "For we all stumble in many ways" (James 3:2). In our homes, we will have a front-row seat to each other's stumblings. We won't pass all the tests, say all the right things, or know all the answers. Sometimes our failures are massive and life-changing. Home is a safe place when we all feel safe to fail, secure in the knowledge that our family will love us even in moments of disappointment.

There is a delicate balance here. We do not want to *encourage* failure—especially when it involves sin. We are not *endorsing* poor behavior in each other. Yet we acknowledge that we all struggle and stumble. In fact, it is so universal so as to be expected (Rom 3:23, 1 Kings 8:46). A safe home is one that does not wink at sin, but also does not treat sin as if it is the end of our relationships.

Safety in this context also does not mean freedom from consequences. Some failures damage trust, cost money, or harm future prospects for success. This is the nature of sin. As parents and spouses, we can't protect each other from consequences. Sometimes (I'm thinking especially here of infidelity or family dishonesty) those failures directly hurt others, so the anger and insecurity they cause is natural. Home, though, is a safe place when we can deal with the fallout of our mistakes while knowing that we still belong.

The night he is betrayed, Jesus both warns and encourages Peter: "Simon, Simon, behold, Satan demanded to have you, that he might sift you like wheat, but I have prayed for you that your faith may not fail. And when you have turned again, strengthen your brothers" (Luke 22:31-32). Jesus knows that Peter will fail this night, denying him three times. He explains that this is part of Satan's work to "sift you like wheat." But Jesus also gives him encouragement: he has prayed for Peter, Peter's faith will not fail, and Peter will "turn again" to future work for Jesus. Peter will fail—and this is disappointing and hurtful—but Jesus will not be done with him.

One of the outstanding pictures of God in the New Testament is as a father whose son has abandoned him, sullied his name, and wasted his money. Yet the son receives this remarkable response upon returning home, humbled and needy: "But while he was still a long way off, his father saw him and felt compassion, and ran and embraced him and kissed him…But the father said to his servants, 'Bring quickly the best robe, and put it on him, and put a ring on his hand, and shoes on his feet. And bring the fattened calf and kill it, and let us eat and celebrate. For this my son was dead, and is alive again; he was lost, and is found'" (Luke 15:20, 22-24). The father welcomes, embraces, and shares gifts with his renegade son. His arms are open, despite the shameful decisions of the past. God is showing us that with him, we are safe to fail, provided we return home to him.

Safety to fail is about more than our initial reactions, though. What is the ongoing fallout when we disappoint and hurt others? Do I keep bringing up that hurtful thing my wife said, even if it was weeks or months ago? Do I brand my children with labels because of their failures—lazy, selfish, angry, rebellious? Do we define ourselves by our mess-ups? Do we define those outside the family by their mess-ups?

As children grow, they will make mistakes. We have patience with them when they are very young (think of a toddler's eating habits), but in time we start to expect more. We want them to make good grades, treat others well, clean up their rooms, and be home by curfew. Yet it is tempting, even as the responsibilities increase, to have less and less patience. Each failure is met with anger while each success is assumed and ignored. Our kids learn that it is not safe to fail.

As we grow in our marriages, we will make mistakes. We have patience with each other when we are just starting, too smitten to be angry for long. But in time we start to expect more. Quirks grow more annoying. Tendencies emerge. Every failure and frustration is magnified. We grow more and more miserable. "A continual dripping on a rainy day and a quarrelsome wife are alike; to restrain her is to restrain the wind or to grasp oil in one's right hand" (Prov 27:15). So we pick at each other. We have long memories of each other's flaws, as if we are preparing for a future court case against our spouse (and sadly, occasionally we are). Our mates learn that it is not safe to fail.

Safety demands a continual, ongoing commitment to patience with one another. I may be disappointed in this moment, but I still love you.

Home is a safe place when we continue to love, forgive, and think the best of one another—even after we fail.

SAFE TO LEARN

Paul charges fathers with teaching their children: "Fathers, do not provoke your children to anger, but bring them up in the discipline and instruction of the Lord" (Eph 6:4). The word translated "instruction" here means to impart understanding, giving children a "mind for" something. Christian homes are founded on the high privilege of teaching our kids to have a heart for Jesus and his way.

In the Jewish mind, this process involves lots of questions. When Jehovah institutes the Passover while Israel is in Egypt, he looks forward: "And when your children say to you, 'What do you mean by this service?' you shall say, 'It is the sacrifice of the LORD's Passover, for he passed over the houses of the people of Israel in Egypt, when he struck the Egyptians but spared our houses'" (Ex 12:26-27). As kids see their parents worshiping and living in a certain way, curiosity is natural. God wants his people to be prepared to engage their children and answer their questions well. These kinds of questions—"what do these stones mean?" (Josh 4:21) or "what is the meaning of the testimonies and the statutes and the rules that the LORD our God has commanded you?" (Deut 6:20)—are not annoyances, but golden opportunities to transmit the faith to the next generation. Christian homes *must* be safe places for us to learn.

James is 4 years old. He has begun to notice some strange things when his parents bring him to church. First, he has to dress in different clothes than normal and comb his hair. Then, he has to be quiet during the service. From time to time he is told to bow his head and close his eyes to pray. Mom and Dad eat a cracker and drink some juice, but he is not allowed to. All of this is mystifying, so he asks about it. But those questions don't come out just right. They sound like, "Dad, why do I have to be still?". They sound like, "I want some juice!". They sound like, "I want to wear my play clothes." His parents' reaction will tell him a lot about this. If Dad responds that all of this is "because I said so!", no learning occurs. "Stop talking in church!" or "just do it!" give the same impression. This doesn't mean that there is not a place to insist on obedience; it is that we very often miss the chances we have to teach. With the best of intentions, we create an environment in which it is unsafe to try to learn.

Children's questions are windows into their hearts. This is what they are thinking about at the moment. Are there dinosaurs in the Bible? Does God ever get sleepy? Why are people so mean? And as they age, their questions age as well. Why are we different from the other families? What should I do for a career? Why did you guys get married? *Their willingness to ask will be a reflection of the safety of the environment we create.*

Meanwhile, our answers to their questions give us space to share our own hearts. There is a touch of the personal even in these old passages about the Mosaic Law. Joshua foresees children asking their parents, "What do these stones mean *to you?*" (Josh 4:6, emphasis mine). Along with the information, we can talk about the feelings that God's things produce in us: The bread represents Jesus' body, which he offered as a sacrifice for us. The fruit of the vine represents his blood, which he shed on the cross. When we eat these things, we think about Jesus. I think about the awful things I have done that caused him to go to the cross for me. I think about how I am living when I remember how much he loved me and wants the best for me. I think about how much he went through. I think about his resurrection and that the cross is not the end. So when I take the LORD's Supper, I feel sad and happy all at once.

In speaking with Christian parents, I have learned that we universally feel a tremendous responsibility to teach our kids and pass the faith on to the next generation. We worry and cry and pray. We create classes, buy books, and ask around. Yet a great deal of our effort and enthusiasm is squandered when we fail to respond to the natural opportunities to learn that come from questions.

Safety to learn will mean that, again, we are patient with one another. Parents need vision that is beyond the frustrations of the moment. Yes, sometimes children are being difficult by asking questions—or by not learning the lesson—but our obligation to teach them still stands. When we correct our children, do they know that we still love and approve of them? Can they bring us the deeper questions of their hearts, knowing that they will be heard and get honest answers?

What home should be is often different from what home actually is. Christian homes should be *safe places*—places where love is shown and we are free to speak, fail, and learn.

For Personal Introspection

- Does my family feel safe around me?
- How has my family of origin contributed to my sense of safety?
- Do I blame others when my home conditions are not ideal?
- Do I ever shut down my mate or children when they express themselves? Why?
- How do I respond when my family members fail? How do they respond when I fail?

For Discussion

- What does a "safe place" mean to you? How do we know when something is unsafe?
- How could a parent provoke a child to anger?
- Why does Paul warn husbands to not be "*harsh*" with their wives? Why are so many of these warnings addressed to men?
- Why do we struggle to make our homes safe places to speak, fail, and learn?
- Would we consider our churches places where it is safe to speak, fail, and learn? Why or why not? If no, how could we change that?

RULE

2

All People Deserve Respect

Some words resist easy definition—and kids seem to ask about them all. *Respect* is such a word. Just take a minute and try it. What is respect? We know it when we see it—or when we *don't* see it—but it is hard to explain it in detail. We recognize that some words, gestures, and behaviors are disrespectful, but we cannot always list out which ones (in which situations) and why it is so. Making respect an integral part of our homes presents a profound challenge.

Marriages hinge on respect. When we feel insulted, dismissed, ignored, condescended to, or shamed, we become deeply unhappy.

Parenting hinges on respect. We teach our children how to listen to, approach, and submit to others. We are preparing our children for engagement with a world full of all kinds of people. Some of them will be respectable—and our kids will need to know how to show them respect. Others will be disreputable—and our kids will need to know how to treat them with courtesy while disagreeing with their actions. Some will be terrible people who are nevertheless in authority over them—as bosses or government officials—and our kids will need to know how to live respectfully anyway.

We learn respect at home.

The contention of this rule is that *all people deserve respect*. When I discuss respect in this rule, I am not referring to those whom we choose to emulate because of the quality of their lives. All people do not deserve *that* respect. Yet in our homes, we must learn that *absolutely all people* deserve a certain level of treatment and kindness from us.

Why?

THEY ARE MADE IN THE IMAGE OF GOD

James teaches us about the pitfalls of our speech by discussing the "tongue."

> With it we bless our LORD and Father, and with it we curse people who are made in the likeness of God. From the same mouth come blessing and cursing. My brothers, these things ought not to be so. Does a spring pour forth from the same opening both fresh and salt water? Can a fig tree, my brothers, bear olives, or a grapevine produce figs? Neither can a salt pond yield fresh water (James 3:9-12).

He highlights the inappropriateness of using our speech to do good one minute, evil the next. We bless God and say kind words about him, then we turn around and curse people and say harsh words against them. Why is this incongruous? People "are made in the likeness of God"! How can we speak well of him and curse the people who are like him?

Of course there is a rich lesson here about how we talk about (and to) others, but James' reasoning is our focus for the moment. His thinking is formed by the creation account:

> Then God said, 'Let us make man in our image, after our likeness. And let them have dominion over the fish of the sea and over the birds of the heavens and over the livestock and over all the earth and over every creeping thing that creeps on the earth.' So God created man in his own image, in the image of God he created him; male and female he created them (Gen 1:27).

If human beings carry the image and likeness of God, there is something inexpressibly great about them. We can never treat any human as if they are less than God's image-bearers.

The precise meaning of the "image of God" has bedeviled Bible students. Opinions abound. Genesis pictures it as (at least) the sense in which all people are distinct from animals (see Gen 1:26, 2:20). Humans have moral consciousness in a way distinct from animals; we know right from wrong, reason through decisions considering the moral dimension, and feel guilt when we do wrong. People can also speak and communicate, carefully (or not so carefully!) articulating our thoughts. We look to the future. We are able to plan, design, and create things. All of these facts make us more like God than like animals.

So James is arguing that *no matter what someone may do—or how much we may feel they deserve our cursing—they deserve respect because they are made in the image of God.* This is distinct from animals. While Scripture teaches us not to be needlessly cruel to animals (Prov 12:10, Deut 25:4), it doesn't particularly matter what we say to them. Our speech to our pets is not "full of deadly poison" (James 3:8). But people are different. Watch what you say to people; they are made in God's image. All the things we will learn about speaking in our homes must be built on this foundation: every single person, no matter what they do, deserves our respect.

People are made in the image of God *even when they are a different race than we are.* There is a shameful history of white Americans (sadly, even Christians) treating black Americans as if they are subhuman—both during and after slavery. The issue is still with us. While we might hope that political change or gradual social development would fix this problem, for Christians, it is a gospel issue. The breeding ground for this kind of racism—and the place where we can bury it—is the home.

We also battle racial resentment toward immigrants. We can become suspicious of them, doubt their motives, and view them as a threat. These visceral emotions—usually driven by fear—can override the clear expectation that we treat foreigners favorably and show hospitality to them (Matt 25:35, Rom 12:13, Heb 13:2, etc). But the greatest danger here is that we *treat them—and talk about them—as if they are less than human*. People of other races are merely people made in the image of God—and our speech about them and treatment of them must always reflect that.

People are made in the image of God *when they have different amounts of money than we do*. Sometimes we treat others condescendingly when they have less than we do. We feel that they are unworthy of our courtesy. James describes a scenario where a wealthy person comes into a Christian assembly and is treated like royalty ("You sit here in a good place") while a poor person is treated shabbily ("you stand over there" or "sit down at my feet") (James 2:2-4). He warns that this makes us "judges with evil thoughts" (James 2:4). Occasionally this goes in the other direction, where we automatically suspect and disdain those who are wealthier. We think the worst about them, criticize their choices, and don't even try to understand them. When we only see people for their clothes and cars (or lack thereof), we dehumanize them. Respect is not an income issue.

People are made in the image of God *whether they are physically attractive or not*. Studies show that we respond much more favorably to good-looking people.[1] Yet Jesus teaches us, "Do not judge by appearances, but judge with right judgment" (John 7:24). In fact, the Bible quite often pictures physical beauty as deceptive: "Like a gold ring in a pig's snout is a beautiful woman without discretion" (Prov 11:22). This doesn't mean we are automatically suspicious of good-looking people either; it means that all people deserve respect,

---

1. Cialdini, p. 148-150. Good-looking Canadian candidates received 2.5 times more votes than unattractive ones. Attractive people are paid 12-14 percent more than their unattractive coworkers. Handsome men receive lighter sentences when defendants in criminal trials. We are more likely to help them and more likely to be persuaded by them. Startlingly, we then maintain that attractiveness has not had any effect on us or our decision-making process.

no matter their outer appearance. Even the unattractive are made in God's image.

People are made in the image of God *even when they believe differently than I do*. Some people will make different faith-choices than I do. I may even disagree with fellow Christians. In fact, some people who are made in the image of God will believe that I am *not* made in the image of God! There will be political differences—parties, opinions about the best policy, what should be on the platform, or how we interpret the Constitution. They may think my beliefs are ridiculous and I may think theirs are. They may be distant from God and in a lost state. But none of this changes the fact that *all people are made in the image of God—and therefore deserve my respect*.

People are made in the image of God *even when their sexual behavior or orientation is not what I believe it should be*. The Bible gives instruction for appropriate sexual behavior, but not everyone recognizes the authority of the Bible. So we will encounter people who have embraced promiscuity, adultery, and homosexuality. How will we treat them? We don't have to respect everyone's choices (who really respects *everyone's* choices?), but they still deserve respect. They are still created in the image of God. No matter what.

THEY HAVE VALUE INDEPENDENT OF HOW THEY TREAT US

Jesus teaches us what respect looks like when people dishonor and hurt us:

> You have heard that it was said, 'An eye for an eye and a tooth for a tooth.' But I say to you, Do not resist the one who is evil. But if anyone slaps you on the right cheek, turn to him the other also. And if anyone forces you to go one mile, go with him two miles. Give to the one who begs from you, and do not refuse the one who would borrow from you (Matt 5:38-42).

Jesus is well aware of the way people often do wrong to one another. He knows that his disciples will at times be the victims of such evil treatment. But he warns against basing our treatment of others on their treatment of us. We cannot just be responders. There is a way that it is right to treat people, no matter how they treat us.

When two NFL or NBA players get frustrated with each other, often one player will instigate conflict and the other will respond. Usually the second player—the responder—will be the one penalized. So it is with Jesus' teaching: the fact that others have acted poorly *never* justifies our response. When others are slapping, forcing, and begging, we don't have to attack! In fact, Jesus tells us to respond to their evil with *kindness*: don't resist, turn the other cheek, go two miles, give, and lend. Why? What is his logic?

> You have heard that it was said, 'You shall love your neighbor and hate your enemy.' But I say to you, Love your enemies and pray for those who persecute you, so that you may be sons of your Father who is in heaven. For he makes his sun rise on the evil and on the good, and sends rain on the just and on the unjust. For if you love those who love you, what reward do you have? Do not even the tax collectors do the same? And if you greet only your brothers, what more are you doing than others? Do not even the Gentiles do the same? You therefore must be perfect, as your heavenly Father is perfect (Matt 5:43-48).

Showing kindness to the undeserving is *God's specialty*. When we show this respect even when others are belligerent, we become "sons of your Father who is in heaven." We become more like him. God knows that there are good and evil people in his world, but his behavior is rooted in his role as Creator. Even when people are disobedient, they are all still dependent on him for life, breath, and all things (Acts 17:25). So he keeps providing: "he makes his sun rise on the evil and on the good, and sends rain on the just and on the unjust." How else will they survive? God doesn't set his watch by how people treat him; there is still a world to run.

He calls his people to this same high standard. After all, what is the alternative? "For if you love those who love you, what reward do you have? Do not even the tax collectors do the same? And if you greet only your brothers, what more are you doing than others? Do not even Gentiles do the same?" These are probing questions. Is our connection to God making any difference in our lives? How much faith does it take to be nice to people who are nice to us? *Everybody* loves those who love them! Is this what we want to pass on to our kids—love your friends and hate everyone else? In what way does that reflect Jesus?

Jesus' words are deeply challenging, yet *this is what we need to be teaching in our homes.* Our kids need to see how their parents react to people who hurt them. They need to see us respond with kindness to our enemies. They need to see us have the courage to *"not resist the one who is evil."* I shudder to think that my children could learn from me to *not* do what Jesus said. *If I am going to have a Christian home, I am going to have to actually follow Jesus.*

Sometimes this happens in real time. We are driving as a family and another car cuts us off, slides into our lane, or runs a stoplight. Anger wells up in me. They are breaking the rules! They are endangering everyone—including *my kids*! I yell out in exclamation, "Hey! What are you doing!". I honk my horn. I glare. Adrenaline flows. These are moments in which I can remember—and demonstrate for my family—that *there is a person in the other car who is made in the image of God.* Perhaps I can find room for compassion ("maybe they're late for something important! Hope they make it!"). Perhaps I can focus on our own family instead of attacking someone else ("Boy, that scared me! Everybody OK?"). What is essential is remembering that in these moments, I am teaching my spouse and children about whether there are times when we don't have to respect other people.

Sometimes the wounds are deeper and the process is slower. People do and say hurtful things to us. Some take advantage of us and damage us financially. They assassinate our reputations, start whisper campaigns, or make moves behind our backs. We may be completely innocent (although some honest self-evaluation is important here), yet we suffer like the guilty. *How will we respond?* The temptation is to fight fire with fire, launching retaliatory attacks against them. Or perhaps our flavor of conflict is to freeze them out, making them feel our anger through cold malice. We may rant and rave, bemoaning their evil to our family and anyone else willing to listen. It will take extraordinary confidence in God to "turn the other cheek" in such situations. Yet these are the scenarios in which faith is tested and character is forged. Our families are watching. They long to learn from us just how deep Christian faith really goes—and how much we truly respect our fellowman.

All people deserve respect because no matter what they do to us, all people have value to God.

THEY HAVE ROLES OF AUTHORITY THAT AFFECT US

No one escapes the reality of authority. As a child, I remember longing for adulthood, when I could go where I wanted (mainly to the movies), eat what I wanted (Fruity Pebbles), and do what I wanted (sleep in and play video games). Yet while I am no longer under the direct authority of my parents, I am still not truly free. All of my actions are constrained by the laws of the nation and state in which I live. While I don't have a typical boss, there are people involved in my work to whom I must answer. As a Christian, I follow the elders at my local church. As a husband and father, I have both authority in my home and a need to submit to the needs and wishes of my family. Translation: I almost never go to the movies, eat Fruity Pebbles, or play video games.

Authority is a fact of life—and we learn it at home. Christians are called to be a *respectful* people.

> Be subject for the LORD's sake to every human institution, whether it be to the emperor as supreme, or to governors as sent by him to punish those who do evil and to praise those who do good. For this is the will of God, that by doing good you should put to silence the ignorance of foolish people. Live as people who are free, not using your freedom as a cover-up for evil, but living as servants of God. Honor everyone. Love the brotherhood. Fear God. Honor the emperor (1 Pet 2:13-17).

We are "subject" to government at all levels—emperors, governors, police. But it is more than angry, reluctant obedience. "Honor everyone…honor the emperor." "Honor" here shows a respectful posture toward others—not only because they are created in God's image, but also because God has given them authority over us.

Paul also makes this connection: "Let every person be subject to the governing authorities. For there is no authority except from God, and those that exist have been instituted by God. Therefore whoever resists the authorities resists what God has appointed, and those who resist will incur judgment" (Rom 13:1-2). It is notable that he writes these words to the Roman Christians, who are living in the shadow of a corrupt empire. They know firsthand the arbitrary and unfair decisions of unstable emperors. It takes some nerve for Paul to equate submission to Nero with submission to God—even calling him "the servant of God" (Rom 13:4) when he is far from it.

Some observations are in order. Neither Paul nor Peter is saying that God specifically chooses certain leaders. They are extolling the *institution of government*. God has given government "for your good" (Rom 13:4). Without government, anarchy would reign and evil would increase. Life would become merely about survival. Without question, some leaders have abused their offices and oppressed their subjects. Yet this doesn't mean government is inherently evil—or that Christians get to throw away the Bible's teaching about submission.

These principles have lasting power because *our focus is never on the rightness of our government, but on our responsibilities to God and others.* "First of all, then, I urge that supplications, prayers, intercessions, and thanksgivings be made for all people, for kings and all who are in high positions, that we may lead a peaceful and quiet life, godly and dignified in every way" (1 Tim 2:1-2). The prayer Paul wants Christians to pray is that the government allow us to live "a peaceful and quiet life." We pray for our leaders—especially that they will continue to leave us alone to live the life Jesus calls us to—and submit to them (provided that their laws do not conflict with God's instructions for us). We might *want* far more from our leaders—we might even be disappointed when they reveal their feet of clay—but our focus remains on our own responsibilities in our homes and communities to serve Jesus and others.

All of this is to say that there is still room for honor and respect for our government and rulers, even when we inevitably disagree with some of their decisions. In fact, it is here that we learn an essential principle: *all the people we must submit to are flawed.* Yet we submit anyway.

Other people are in charge over us. "Servants, be subject to your masters with all respect, not only to the good and gentle but also to the unjust" (1 Pet 2:18). Thankfully, slavery has been mostly eradicated in our time. Yet we still must submit to others who are in positions of authority over us—whether in our workplaces or community organizations or sports teams or classrooms. Some will be "good and gentle" while others will be "unjust." Either way we can follow them "with all respect."

Paul instructs married couples: "Let each one of you love his wife as himself, and let the wife see that she respects her husband"

(Eph 5:33). He does not merely stress submission here (as he does a few verses earlier in 5:22-24), but respect.

Paul instructs Christians in a local church: "We ask you, brothers, to respect those who labor among you and are over you in the LORD and admonish you, and to esteem them very highly in love because of their work" (1 Thess 5:12-13). This probably refers to the elders with their local church. Following them and submitting to their decisions is important; respect is a different issue. They deserve for us to "respect" them and "esteem them very highly in love because of their work." They are in authority over us and this is a blessing, so we esteem them highly even if we disagree with some of the specifics of their decisions.

So many passages teach us to respect authority that it is impossible to miss the trend. There are people who are in authority over us, no matter how old we get. We submit to them and honor them. They will make some decisions that we disagree with. They will occasionally make poor moral choices. *They still deserve respect.* This is a lesson learned at home.

This is the context in which parent/child dynamics are described in Scripture. "Children, obey your parents in the LORD, for this is right. 'Honor your father and mother' (this is the first commandment with a promise), 'that it may go well with you and that you may live long in the land'" (Eph 6:1-3). The expectation that we will obey and honor *starts with our parents*. This is where we first learn what respect means. This is where we learn how to submit when we don't agree. This is where we learn the key skills of teamwork, obedience, and perseverance.

The Hebrew writer also draws on our submission to our parents as a pattern for our submission to God. "Besides this, we have had earthly fathers who disciplined us and we respected them. Shall we not much more be subject to the Father of spirits and live?" (Heb 12:9). Children's respect for their parents is *assumed*. Yet just as we treated our parents respectfully, so we *trust and obey our heavenly*

Father. The implications are massive. If, as children, we have not learned how to respect and obey our parents, we will struggle to submit our hearts to God. We won't know how. If, as parents, we have not taught our children to respect authority, they will struggle to respect God.

WHAT DOES RESPECT LOOK LIKE?

If all people deserve respect, then it will become the expected tone of our home. How do we show and teach respect?

> *Respect is very commonly shown in our speech.*

We show disrespect when we insult and tear down others (whether they are present or absent). Some modes of address show respect; for example, we often don't use first names of older people or teachers. Many ways we communicate respect in speech are cultural or regional. I've already mentioned that I was raised to address adults as "sir" or "ma'am" as a sign of respect. But even though there is some variation, *we know disrespect when we see it*. Ignoring others, greeting questions with silence, or refusing to speak when we're angry are usually disrespectful. Some tones of voice (mocking, angry, dismissive) are disrespectful. Refusing to make eye contact can be. The list can go on and on—and needs to be adapted from family to family.

This is especially pertinent when husbands and wives speak disrespectfully about people outside the family. When we make racial jokes and broad racial judgments, we show that some entire groups are unworthy of the simple respect of being judged on their own merits. It matters what we say about people who have hurt us, disappointed us, or frustrated us. *Can we still speak respectfully about them?* Meanwhile, our disrespectful attitudes affect our spouses, who can get caught up in our negativity with us. And all the while our children are listening carefully, wondering what mistakes *they might make* that would cause their parents to completely disrespect them. They are also learning in what situations they should be as ruthless as their parents are.

Respect is shown in how we interact with people.

James criticizes Christians who would give places of honor and lots of attention to the wealthy while giving short shrift to the poor. The rich are shown respect by where they sit. He fumes: "But you have dishonored the poor man" (James 2:6). Often we give more of our attention to the attractive while ignoring the less attractive; this is disrespect. Paul wants Christians to "show perfect courtesy toward all people" (Titus 3:2). In our society we sometimes speak of "common courtesy," the basic sense of respect we show each other. *Our kids must be taught what common courtesy is.*

In closer relationships, there are interactions that signal a deeper respect. When a husband "(shows) honor" (1 Pet 3:7) to his wife, he speaks well of her, pays attention to her, thinks about her when she is not around, refuses to insult her, does kind things for her, seeks to understand her, and acts in her best interest. When a wife "respects her husband" (Eph 5:33), she goes along with his decisions, encourages him, praises him to others, and works together with him for the betterment of the family. Notice that respect and honor are not role-specific; everyone shows respect and everyone deserves respect.

Respect is even important in dealing with our kids. Are we aware of our children's feelings? Do we hear their side of the story before reacting? Do we allow them to speak? These are simple measures of respect we would grant to almost everyone else; why would we have less respect for our children? Do we tailor our discipline and instruction to what is best for them? Meanwhile, children also must show respect to their parents—trusting their judgment, accepting their authority, and appreciating the difficulty of their task.

Some words resist easy definition—but that does not mean they are unimportant. Christian homes should be places steeped in respect for all people. *All people deserve respect.*

For Personal Introspection

- Whom do I have the hardest time respecting?
- Do I want the respect of others? What are some ways I feel disrespected?
- Do I ever seek others' respect while not giving respect to others?
- How might I respond respectfully to people who hurt me? What are the limits of respect in that situation?
- Who is in authority over me? What are those relationships like?

For Discussion

- How does the claim of this rule that "all people deserve respect" strike you? Are there people whom you believe don't deserve respect?
- Is respect earned? How do we give respect to people whom we feel have not earned it? Should we?
- What does it mean to be created "in the image of God"? Why is it hard to remember this when we deal with people?
- How might I show respect to the government? How does the New Testament's teaching on government challenge the modern American political climate?
- What are some methods for teaching respect in the home?

RULE

3

We Tell the Truth

"You shall not bear false witness against your neighbor." (Exodus 20:16)

We are in the back half of the Ten Commandments here—where God's rules turn from our dealings with *him* to our dealing with *other people*. He has never intended religion to be a strictly private, internal affair. Our moral choices take place in an interconnected world where we necessarily affect other people. Our impulses, desires, emotions, and decisions can help or hurt, bless or curse.

So he tells us to *tell the truth*.

Bearing false witness has a particular context. It takes us to the ancient "courtroom" of Israel, where facts are established on the testimony of two or three witnesses (Deut 19:15). To lie about what we have seen is to falsely condemn our neighbor. It is a lie with consequences. Yet *all* our efforts at honesty—all of our words—are about *bearing witness to what we believe is true*. We have a testimony to give. We testify to the truth of the world as we know it. We bear witness about the facts of a situation, the emotions we are feeling, or what we know about others. And when called to testify, Christians do not bear false witness. *We tell the truth.*

What does telling the truth look like in our homes?

WHEN WE TALK ABOUT OTHERS—AND OURSELVES

God warns against false witness because of its tremendous potential to damage others. When we testify to something that is not true, others begin to operate as if it is true. A person is convicted on our testimony. Character is assassinated. Lives are ruined. Dishonesty has victims.

This is one reason why Paul instructs new Christians about their need to rethink this part of their speech. "Therefore, having put away falsehood, let each one of you speak the truth with his neighbor, for we are members one of another" (Eph 4:25). "Falsehood" is part of the "old self" (Eph 4:22). Coming to Jesus means that we have abandoned our old habit of playing fast and loose with the truth to gain advantage. We serve a God who tells the truth (John 17:17) and cannot lie (Titus 1:2). Satan is the father of lies (John 8:44).

Yet Paul says we tell the truth because "we are members one of another." This introduces a new dimension. Others (our "neighbor") deserve the truth from us. Lying hurts them because we are connected to them—and dishonesty has victims.

I don't believe we need extensive biblical proof of the idea. *Everyone acknowledges that lying is wrong in most situations.* Movies, TV shows, and novels—most of which are created by people who are not Christians—use dishonesty as a plot wrinkle. The tension comes from a moment when someone lies or withholds the truth from someone close to them. What will happen? Will the truth come out? Will the relationship survive? This draws us in because we recognize that *lying is a betrayal.*

Yet my experience with my kids has shown me that I need to be more specific about my meaning here. Not everyone deserves this level of extreme honesty from us. There are some people we cannot trust, with whom complete transparency would be inappropriate. This means that Christians need to learn and develop the skill of wisely discerning what information is pertinent, relevant, and deserved—without lying.

For example, if someone asks my young daughter where her parents are, she doesn't always need to answer. If someone asks my young son if he has a crush on anyone, he does not always need to fully disclose his heart to them. Some people are not trustworthy, while others are not close enough to have a claim on our deepest thoughts. So while we need to ask whether this person is worthy of our confidence, *we don't just lie. Trust—or the lack thereof—is not an excuse to just lie to everyone.*

And if there is anyone we can completely trust, it should be our families. Home is a safe place.

But honesty is also a part of our speech as regards *ourselves*. There is a whole inner world within each of us—a whirlwind of desires, emotions, pains, hopes, beliefs, and expectations. While others may be able to read some of our internal life through our actions, they never know the truth of it—unless we tell them. "For who knows a person's thoughts except the spirit of that person, which is in him?" (1 Cor 2:11). Paul has a different point in mind here—about God's revelation of his *own* mind through his Spirit—yet he reasons from a simple principle: no one knows exactly what we are thinking except ourselves.

And God expects us to be honest in what we tell others about what we are thinking and feeling. "O LORD, who shall sojourn in your tent? Who shall dwell on your holy hill? He who walks blamelessly and does what is right and speaks truth in his heart" (Psalm 15:1-2). The one who pleases God and is allowed to live with him is the one "speaks truth in his heart." One commentator says of this verse, "truth means what is sure and trustworthy, not merely correct. What this man says is one with what he is."[1] God wants people who are *true*—who are precisely what they say they

---

1. Kidner, in loc.

are. This demands that we be truthful when we talk about ourselves. David, in his emotional prayer of repentance, confesses to God: "Behold, you desire truth in the inward being, and you teach me wisdom in the secret heart" (Psalm 51:6). Truth—deep down, on the inside, in the heart—is what forms Christian men and women. When he describes the wicked, he declares that "there is no truth in their mouth; their inmost self is destruction" (Psalm 5:9). When we speak—about others or ourselves—we speak from our "inmost self" and draw on our inner reservoir of truth.

The implications here are important. When things are bothering us, challenging us, consuming us, or exciting us, we need to be able to be honest, especially with those we are closest to. When we conceal our thoughts and feelings, sinister desires can grow, hurts can deepen, and anger can fester. Then these emotions create distance between us and our confused spouses and children. They learn that they must hide the truth of their own hearts.

Christian homes must be different. Home is a safe place, where we learn to tell the truth about others and ourselves.

WHEN WE ARE WRONG

It is a particularly humbling experience to have to admit that we are wrong. We fight it. We long to explain our precise reasoning, the environmental factors, and why we felt it was necessary. Sometimes we try to blame the person accusing us: they took our words out of context, they took it seriously when we were joking, or they are too sensitive.

Christian homes should be places where we tell the truth about being wrong.

This tendency to cover up and deny has a long history. Adam blames Eve for his own choice to eat the fruit. Aaron blames the people for his own decision to make a golden calf. Saul blames the people for his own disobedience. John warns that it continues with us: "If we say we have no sin, we deceive ourselves, and the truth is not in us. If we confess our sins, he is faithful and just to forgive us our sins and to cleanse us from all unrighteousness. If we say we have not sinned, we make him a liar, and his word is not in us" (1 John 1:8-10). John zeroes in on what we *say* about our sin. He has in mind our pattern of life (rather than particular sins), but our pattern of life is merely the composite of our reactions to all the times we sin. This means that admitting sin, confessing it, and turning away from it is *something that Christians will practice with regularity*. We will become deeply familiar with the process and the terminology. We will learn to say we are sorry. We will learn to tell others what we struggle with. We will tell the truth.

When God calls Peter to preach about Jesus for the first time to Gentiles, he takes some convincing. He has a repetitive vision. The Spirit speaks to him. Some men arrive from a Roman named Cornelius, asking Peter to come to his house because he has been visited by angel. When he goes and speaks to them, the Holy Spirit descends on Cornelius and his friends and they begin to speak in tongues. Only after all that does Peter finally conclude that these people can become Christians too.

But when the other Jewish Christians hear about it, they are upset. Peter explains the entire situation in detail, going through each angelic appearance and movement of the Spirit up to the baptism of the first Gentile converts. I find the next verse one of the most amazing and powerful in all of the Bible. "When they heard these things they fell silent. And they glorified God, saying, 'Then to the Gentiles also God has granted repentance that leads to life'" (Acts 11:18). First they "(fall) silent." They do not argue or defend their long-held belief that Jews and Gentiles have no part together. They do not reject Peter or attack his testimony. They hold their tongues. They think it through. They ask themselves the fateful question: *what if I am wrong?* Then they praise God and *tell the truth*: God has accepted Gentiles. *I was wrong about that. But now I accept the truth about it.*

This combination of boldness and humility is the kind of talk Christians need to base their homes on. We own our mistakes. We confess our weaknesses. This is hard. It will humble us. We will lower our voices and hang our heads a bit as we say it. But honesty demands that there be a moment where we drop the denials, justifications, and arguments. *I'm sorry. I shouldn't have done that. I was wrong. Can you forgive me?*

WHEN WE MAKE COMMITMENTS

Paul lists "faithfulness" as one of the fruits of the Spirit (Gal 5:22). This is distinct from *faith*—where we believe something about God. It is more closely related to *fidelity* or *trustworthiness*. It speaks to our willingness to do what we have committed to. Are we people who can be trusted to follow through on their commitments—or are we liars?

Jesus excoriates religious leaders who only keep their word when they have sworn by a certain thing (Matt 23:16). They split hairs and pick nits to create loopholes so that they can break their word. We all know people whose commitment we cannot trust even if it is writing. Jesus calls us to a higher honesty.

Faithfulness is a fruit of the Spirit because it is a fundamental characteristic of God. It is who he is. "God is faithful" (1 Cor 1:9). "God is faithful" (1 Cor 10:13). "He who calls you is faithful" (1 Thess 5:24). "But the LORD is faithful" (2 Thess 3:3). These passages are only a sampling; there are more. The entirety of our faith hinges on the certainty that God will do what he has promised; without this, we have nothing. He would not lie to us and if he failed to keep his word, we would view it as a lie.

So Christian homes must become places where we train one another to keep our word. We do what we said we would do. We meet our responsibilities. We show up where we say we will. We are dependable and straightforward. This necessarily means that we are careful before we make commitments. We don't want to make frivolous commitments because we want our word to mean something. We think carefully about our ability to actually do what we plan.

And with this diligence and determination about daily commitments, we lay the groundwork for the bigger commitments. Husbands and wives commit to one another for life, never allowing the pressures and frustrations of the moment to annul their faithfulness to that commitment. The strength of this bond becomes the foundation of the home. We go to work when we don't feel like it. We serve others even when we're out of gas. We keep following Jesus, in season and out of season, because we have committed to him.

In my seventh grade year, I committed to playing football. I hated it from the first practice. Since it was Texas in August, it was hot. I was small. I couldn't tackle. I couldn't throw the ball. I couldn't move the tackling dummy. The coaches yelled at me constantly, challenging my manhood. Everything smelled bad. I drew up a calendar to count down the days until the season ended, crossing off day after agonizing day. I was thoroughly miserable. But when I mentioned to my mom the possibility of quitting, she refused to let me. I had committed to play, so I was going to play through the whole season. I wish I could say that I made peace with football and found my groove, but I didn't. I hated every last minute of it. But to this day, I do not make commitments lightly. Spending 100 days trapped in a prison of my own making has made me careful and intentional. Breaking my word is not an option.

Children raised in this environment learn the enduring power of faithfulness. They think carefully and soberly about their own major decisions—marriages, careers, and spiritual life. They are formed to be like God—faithful. They tell the truth.

WHY ARE WE AFRAID TO TELL THE TRUTH?

As we think about creating an atmosphere of truth-telling in our homes, it will help us to consider why it is so challenging.

There might be consequences.

I noticed this early on in my parenting. At a very young age, children learn the basics of self-preservation. "Did you eat the cookie?", after a certain age, will almost certainly get a "no" response. As soon as the child realizes that the truth will lead to trouble, truth becomes a scary thing. Yet as we grow, the same basic impulse only grows more sophisticated. We become more accomplished liars because we desperately want to avoid the punishment that comes from admitting we have disobeyed. Truth-telling may mean paying more on our taxes, admitting to the officer what we did, or getting grounded for breaking the rules.

We don't want to disappoint or anger others.

It is not always punishment that we fear. Honesty is a struggle when we see the collateral damage it causes to our relationships. As we learn the difference in the severity of a mistake (eating the cookie vs. wrecking the car), we find it so unpleasant to upset and frustrate those we care about that we cover up what we have done. The fallacy here is that it is somehow noble to withhold information from others if it would upset them.

We fear we'll lose love.

Taken further, our fear of the truth comes from the possibility that if people know all that we have done or thought, they will not love us anymore. We view love as a finite quantity—when we mess up, we make a withdrawal from our account. Is it possible that full disclosure would leave our account overdrawn? If you know my rap sheet, my true opinions, my sexual history, or my greatest embarrassment, you might see how unworthy I am of your love. If I have dark secrets in my past, harbor evil emotions or intentions, or feel things I fear others wouldn't approve of, I hide. If we limit what others know about us, we think that we can obscure the less flattering parts of our hearts.

We develop a habit of dishonesty and evasion.

When we lie about something, we back ourselves into a corner the next time it comes up. Can we tell the truth now? We get used to lying. We get better at it. We change subjects. We lie straight-faced. At some point, coming clean becomes such a massive project that we assume we could never do it.

In establishing a truth-telling home, these are the battles we must fight. There *are* consequences when we tell the truth that we have done something bad. No amount of parental coddling can (or should) protect us from that. Yet here is our battle: promoting honesty while assuring our mates and children that truth will not cause us to love them less or permanently disenchant us.

A PATH TOWARD A TRUTH-TELLING HOME

How do we get there?

Tell the truth.

This starts with parents and spouses. We cannot expect honesty from our kids when they never see it from us. We cannot expect honesty from our spouse if we don't practice it ourselves. A consistent habit of truth-telling in small things ("I'm sorry I didn't take the trash out. I forgot") and large things ("I'm wondering if we need to move") shows those around us that we can be relied on to be honest. They will know us as a straight shooter—not in the sense of being insensitive, but dependably truthful. We show our spouses and children that *sometimes telling the truth costs us—but that we accept the costs and tell the truth anyway.* No amount of parenting strategy can ever replace personal honesty and integrity.

Own your mistakes and overreactions.

We will not be perfect as spouses or parents. We need to be able to admit when we are wrong. We will have poor responses to people and events, raise our voices inappropriately, and misjudge situations. *It is quite valuable for our spouses and children to hear us admit this.* Our kids are not the only ones who are imperfect. I know that the fear here is that this will diminish our influence, yet I disagree in the strongest possible terms. Honesty humanizes us to our children and shows them the humility we are trying to teach them. No one is above the law. *If we want our kids to tell the truth when they are wrong, how can we not?*

Balance truth and age-appropriateness.

Sometimes kids ask questions that are above their pay grade. After one move, my kids (at the time ages 8, 7, and 4) wanted to know how much our house cost. Since they had little awareness of money and probably would have told everyone they knew, I declined to answer the question. Children may ask about anatomy or reproduction at a time when they are not old enough for a sex ed class. Lots of these questions ("where do babies come from?", "is Santa Claus real?") are deeply challenging to answer in an age-appropriate way. *We must deal with these matters without lying to our kids.* There are a range of answers that find this balance—from "I'll tell you when you're older" to general explanations omitting delicate details. It is also important to dig down a little deeper to discover a child's true intent with a question. I know of a parent who, when asked by a young child the meaning of the word "gay," responded reluctantly with an extended description of "when boys like boys." Only afterward did the parent learn that the child was asking about the use of the word to mean "happy."

Be careful about punishing honesty.

If we punish our children when they admit they took the cookie, what are we teaching? Wouldn't any reasonable child learn that more honesty leads to worse punishments than denial? I'm not arguing that everything is acceptable as long as we are honest about it. Instead, I'm concerned about incentivizing a behavior (dishonesty) that we are not trying to teach. We have tried to make it a rule in our home that it is always better to be honest, even if we have done wrong. It is important to attempt to make punishments reflect that.

Be honest with and trusting of your mate.

Truth-telling homes have open, honest conversation between spouses. If we have children, they need to know that their parents talk to and know each other very well. We share information. We trust each other. We are on the same team.

Honest mates know each other's passwords and internet history. We are unafraid to share where we have been and what we have been doing. We share whom we have been talking to and how it makes us feel. There is a twofold obligation here: to be willing to share honestly and to be willing to receive honest words.

Jim has worked in a small business for 15 years. Recently his boss has hired a new lower-level employee, Amber. Amber is a very attractive younger woman. Over the last few months, as he and Amber have interacted more often, they have begun to flirt in a light-hearted manner. Amber makes jokes at his expense (she makes fun of his fashion sense) and he has started teasing her back (he thinks she uses her phone too much). Jim has recently noticed that he feels a little bit of excitement when he thinks about seeing Amber each day. She is a nice person and they get along well.

Jim is torn. He is happily married and is not interested in having an affair. But he is honest enough to acknowledge that he is developing feelings for Amber. Heaviest on his mind is the question of whether he should tell his wife, Melissa, about this. Does she deserve to know this? Won't it just upset her unnecessarily? Surely, Jim feels, he won't act on any of this! And besides, nothing has really happened anyway! For someone in Jim's position, honesty takes a great deal of trust, wisdom, and passion for moral purity.

Meanwhile, what will Melissa say? Surely if Jim comes to her and mentions his growing feelings for a younger woman, it will hurt her. She will have lots of questions about the specifics of what has happened to this point. Yet, when all the facts are on the table, Melissa also has an obligation to receive Jim's honesty well. She can acknowledge that she is hurt and upset by the information, but that she also appreciates knowing the situation.

Now Jim and Melissa can sit down together and brainstorm how to manage a difficult situation. Because there is honesty, they know that they are both interested in saving their marriage and preventing a problem. Does Jim need to quit? Should someone say something to Amber? Would it help to have a regular time of accountability about this relationship? Should we find ways to limit time alone? Now we have two aligned family members solving a problem that threatens the integrity of the family. *Solutions like this can only happen if we are honest and trusting of one another.*

Honesty also means that my spouse deserves to know what I am looking at and doing online. Smartphones and tablets have made many great advances for us, but they have also made pornography more convenient, portable, and tempting than ever before. Marriages can survive pornography, but not if we ignore it. Initiating these conversations—which should be happening in every Christian home—will require great courage. Responding in honesty will require great courage. Hearing hard truths will require great courage. Leaning in to the marriage and choosing to work with my mate through a problem like pornography is a long and hard road. But in Christian homes, *we tell the truth.*

Keep your word and your promises.

When we make commitments to one another, truth-telling will mean that we follow through. Promises must be made very carefully and thoughtfully. *Do what you say.*

Each of us has a witness to bear. In our homes, we are creating a culture—either of consistent honesty or of playing fast and loose with the truth. Christian homes are bastions of extreme honesty. *We tell the truth.*

For Personal Introspection

- In what situations am I tempted to be dishonest? What am I thinking?
- Am I willing to talk about my anxieties, feelings, and disappointments? Why am I sometimes hesitant to open up?
- When was the last time I admitted I was wrong?
- Am I reliable in keeping my commitments? Do I say yes to too many things?
- How is my honesty with my mate? My kids?

For Discussion

- What is the difference between honesty and openness?
- What are some examples of people who don't deserve full disclosure from us? Who are some people we should be more open with?
- Is being honest about our own hearts exclusively feminine? Is this important? Why is it challenging for men?
- What makes an apology sincere?
- What makes someone dependable?
- How should we handle situations where our children ask questions that are not age-appropriate?
- What other suggestions would you make for creating a truth-telling home?

RULE 4

We Speak with Love

Sometimes small things matter a lot. A little mustard seed becomes a large tree. A little dash of leaven makes a big impact on a loaf of bread. James teaches us to think this way about our speech. It seems like a small thing—how big is our tongue compared to, say, our leg?—yet it is hugely important.

"If we put bits into the mouths of horses so that they obey us, we guide their whole bodies as well. Look at the ships also: though they are so large and are driven by strong winds, they are guided by a very small rudder wherever the will of the pilot directs. So also the tongue is a small member, yet it boasts of great things. How great a forest is set ablaze by such a small fire!" (James 3:3-5). A small bit controls a horse. A small rudder controls a ship. And a small tongue controls the course of our relationship with others and service to God.

James is particularly concerned with the outsized potential for disaster in the tongue. "How great a forest is set ablaze by such a small fire! And the tongue is a fire, a world of unrighteousness…It is a restless evil, full of deadly poison" (James 3:5-6, 8). Our words wound and sting. Every person holds, etched in their memories, the scars of hurtful things said to them. We remember the words even when the person who said them is dead or far distant. "You'll never amount to anything!". "You need to lose weight." "You're a loser just like your dad." "I hate you!". The alarming truth is that the people with the greatest potential to cause this kind of long-lasting pain with their words are those who live with us.

He also compares the tongue to a wild animal. "For every kind of beast and bird, of reptile and sea creature, can be tamed and has been tamed by mankind, but no human being can tame the tongue. It is a restless evil, full of deadly poison" (James 3:7-8). Over time, animals can grow accustomed to being around people. Eventually you can trust them not to bite or attack you. You can take off the leash. *That's never true with the tongue.* There is no point at which we can take off the leash and just "let it rip." Even when we feel extremely comfortable with someone, if we lose our filter, the consequences will be disastrous. This is true even when we are with our families.

We want our homes to be safe places—nurturing, warm, and loving. We want our homes to be filled with positive memories.

We speak with love.

WE SHOW KINDNESS INSTEAD OF HARSHNESS

God's character is marked by an undeserved kindness toward his creation. "But love your enemies, and do good, and lend, expecting nothing in return, and your reward will be great, and you will be sons of the Most High, for he is kind to the ungrateful and evil" (Luke 6:35). God continues to give life—and even good things!—to those who spurn him. He is *kind*—and Jesus urges us to be like him. This is the reason that kindness is one of the fruits of the Spirit (Gal 5:22). When God's Spirit is at work in our hearts, helping us grow into the image of Jesus, we grow kinder.

So if kindness is our baseline, then how much more can we show kindness to the people in our families, with whom we share a much deeper connection?

When Paul describes the nature of love, though, note how many of these attributes are things we *say*.

> Love is patient and kind; love does not envy or boast; it is not arrogant or rude. It does not insist on its own way; it is not irritable or resentful; it does not rejoice at wrongdoing, but rejoices with the truth. Love bears all things, believes all things, hopes all things, endures all things (1 Cor 13:4-7).

Patience and kindness are usually shown by our words rather than our actions. In fact, they are often evidenced in the *tone of voice* in which we address others. A hard truth told in a soft tone shows kindness, but a benign statement in an exasperated tone communicates impatience. If "love does not boast," then our speech will not be solely focused on ourselves and our own greatness. We will speak positively about others. Being "arrogant or rude" is usually a speech matter. Irritation—or being "easily provoked"—is expressed verbally. Running throughout the entire passage is that love is primarily concerned about the other person, not ourselves. That is communicated through speech. *If we want to show love, we will have to learn how to* speak *with love.*

Kindness clashes powerfully with the harshness that Paul warns against. We have spoken extensively about Paul's challenge to Christian husbands and fathers to not provoke their children (Col 3:21, Eph 6:4) and not to be bitter or harsh with their wives (Col 3:19). The arena in which kindness and harshness plays out is in how we talk to each other. Words have a power even if the words themselves are not hurtful. Often the power is in our tone. We can communicate anger, disappointment, shame, and hatred by our tone. *What is my tone communicating to my family about how I feel about them?*

Sometimes our familiarity with our families leads us to loosen the leash on our tongues. We speak out of raw emotions and wound them. We do not take time to consider the impact of our words. We get frustrated, tired, or stressed and take it out on each other. Sometimes we even blame others ("you're just too sensitive!") when we are the ones who are being unkind. *Would I be speaking to my family the same way if I wasn't feeling what I'm feeling?*

Kindness does not mean that we always agree with our spouses or children. It does not mean that there are never any consequences for foolish actions. It does not mean that we always accept how we are being treated. *It means that I temper my anger and rage because God has taught me to speak kindly.* Maybe I need to take time before I speak. Maybe I need to reformulate what I am saying so that my family hears my point instead of my anger. Maybe different wording, a softer voice, or a different venue would help. Maybe I just need to calm down. *Am I speaking kindly or harshly?*

WE BUILD UP INSTEAD OF INSULTING

James points out an inconsistency in how we use our tongue.

> With it we bless our LORD and Father, and with it we curse people who are made in the likeness of God. From the same mouth come blessing and cursing. My brothers, these things ought not to be so. Does a spring pour forth from the same opening both fresh and salt water? Can a fig tree, my brothers, bear olives, or a grapevine produce figs? Neither can a salt pond yield fresh water (James 3:9-12).

We bless God—saying wonderful, positive things about him and what he has done for us—and then we curse people—saying horrible, negative things about them and what they have done to us. How can this be? How can we use our mouths one minute to praise and the next to insult? All of his illustrations—springs and trees and ponds—tell us that this is completely unnatural. My brothers, these things ought not to be so.

But James is pointing us in the direction of consistency. *We should use our tongues to praise others just like we praise God.* Disparaging and insulting others just doesn't fit with what we know about God. Christians should be a people whose speech is consistently pure and kind, not full of insults and curses against others. We talk about them the way we talk about God. Nowhere is this more important than in our homes.

Paul teaches us to let our speech reflect Jesus' speech (his "word"): "Let the word of Christ dwell in you richly, teaching and admonishing one another in all wisdom, singing psalms and hymns and spiritual songs, with thankfulness in your hearts to God" (Col 3:16). What comes out of our mouths is determined by what we allow to dwell in our hearts (see Matt 12:33-37). When we let Jesus' words live in us, we are full of good words for others. We have things to teach, admonishment to give, songs to sing, and loving gratitude to express. These are the sentiments that permeate Christian homes. We are full of gratitude and patience and wisdom and song. We speak with love.

Paul pushes us to subject our speech to an even higher standard. "Let no corrupting talk come out of your mouths, but only such as is good for building up, as fits the occasion, that it may give grace to those who hear" (Eph 4:29). "Building up" here is a word for constructing a building. We would say that our speech needs to be *constructive*. The image is that by our words and interactions, each day we are adding to someone else's "building." Are we benefiting those around us by our speech? Have we added a brick of faith, confidence, hope, strength, or encouragement? Or have we torn down what confidence or positivity they had? Have we corrupted or disheartened?

This verse shifts our paradigm. Speaking is not about venting ("I can't believe you did that! What are you thinking?") or insulting ("you're such an idiot!") or expressing ourselves ("I just hate this!"). *We must learn to think about the impact of our words—every word, all the time.* Are my words "corrupting" or "good for building up"? *Do my words give grace?*

Many hurtful words are insulting because *they label a person rather than addressing a behavior.* Branding someone as lazy, selfish, ugly, stupid, a loser, or weak is particularly harmful because these terms describe something we *are*. It is an assault on character that cannot be easily changed. It's just who I am. Such words provide no path to growth. No matter how much I study, I will still be stupid. No matter how much I show strength, I will still worry that I am weak. No matter how much I serve others, I will still revert to selfishness. When we talk to others (especially our spouses and kids) this way, we brand them with soul-scars that never go away. Speaking with love means that we will keep the focus on what a person has done. "You didn't work very hard on this assignment" is preferable to "you're lazy"; "that shirt is not very flattering" is better than "you look bad"; "I want you to consider how that makes your sister feel" is superior to "you're so selfish."

The undercurrent of the Christian home is that *I love you and want to build you up.* Insults never express love and do not build up. We speak with love.

WE DISAGREE AND CORRECT INSTEAD OF ATTACKING

Speaking with love does not mean that we have to agree with everything others say and do. We will not always see eye to eye with spouses and will regularly need to correct our children. Even children will protest the judgments of their parents—and we have already argued that they should be free to respectfully do so. But *love has a way of disagreeing that does not attack.*

When Paul is preparing Timothy for his preaching work, he stresses the need for discernment. "Have nothing to do with foolish, ignorant controversies; you know that they breed quarrels. And the LORD's servant must not be quarrelsome but kind to everyone, able to teach, patiently enduring evil, correcting his opponents with gentleness. God may perhaps grant them repentance leading to a knowledge of the truth, and they may come to their senses and escape from the snare of the devil, after being captured by him to do his will" (2 Tim 2:23-26). There are some kinds of controversies that do no good and only make people argue with each other ("foolish, ignorant controversies" that "breed quarrels"). I might add here that this is not only true in religious matters. We tend to get sidetracked into foolish arguments in all areas of life. We want to win an argument—even if it's only an argument about the best food or sports team or place to live—and often alienate the person we are arguing with. Paul's advice for Timothy's preaching is sound advice for Christian homes: *pick your battles*.

But as Timothy pursues love (2 Tim 2:22), Paul reminds him not to be "quarrelsome but kind to everyone." Don't just go looking for fights. Not everyone is your enemy. Instead, be the type of person who "(corrects) his opponents with gentleness." Be kind. Show love. Disagree with them (they are your *opponents!*), but you don't have to attack them.

Timothy will see many things that he disagrees with. "Preach the word; be ready in season and out of season; reprove, rebuke, and exhort, with complete patience and teaching" (2 Tim 4:2). He should be willing to correct at all times, but approach people "with complete patience and teaching." We can correct, reprove, and rebuke others in love. This is a vital skill in a Christian home.

Love *focuses on the substance of what we disagree about, not attacking the person.* I can disagree with you and still love you (in fact, I'm pretty sure we all disagree about something). I can disapprove of your behavior without accusing you of being a terrible person. Parents can disagree with their children—and correct them—without attacking them personally. Children can disagree with their parents without attacking them personally. We express ourselves clearly, but still understand that our parents are in control and we all love each other. *There is a line there that love does not cross.*

17 year-old Jill's curfew is 11:00 PM, yet she is out until 12:15 AM. She tries to come in quietly and not wake anyone up, but she finds her dad waiting for her in the living room. How will this conversation play out?

Option 1

DAD: Where have you been?

JILL: I was just out with my friends and I lost track of time. Sorry!

DAD: I can't believe you didn't tell us what was happening! I texted you and you never responded. Your mother's been worried sick. I just can't believe how inconsiderate you are!

JILL: Dad! I didn't text you back because by the time I saw your message it was too late. But I didn't want to text you back because you always get mad about everything! I wasn't even doing anything wrong!

DAD: Oh, so now this is my fault? That's just like you! You never think about anyone but yourself!

JILL: You're just mad because you always have to be in control of everything. Heaven forbid your daughter has an innocent good time with her friends.

DAD: You don't talk to me like that! I can't believe how disrespectful you are! I didn't raise you like that! Go to your room!

Option 2

DAD: Where have you been? We were worried.

JILL: I was just out with my friends and I lost track of time. Sorry!

DAD: Why didn't you answer my text?

JILL: I saw it a while after you sent it, but by that time I was already heading back home.

DAD: What were you guys doing?

JILL: We were just watching a movie at Angela's house.

DAD: So when we set up a curfew, you agreed to 11:00, right?

JILL: Yes. I just wanted to stay out a little while longer, so I guess I wasn't watching the clock very closely.

DAD: Part of the reason we have a curfew is so that we know that you're safe at night. When you don't let us know what's going on, we don't know if you're safe.

JILL: I know, Dad. I'm sorry.

DAD: If you had texted us to let us know, we might have let you stay out longer. But now I don't see that I have any choice but to punish you. You've broken our agreement. What do you think a fair punishment would be?

JILL: Oh, Dad, I don't know. You decide.

DAD: I think you should be grounded in the evenings for a week. I want you to remember that when we make an agreement, we keep our word or at least let others know when we can't. (Hugs Jill). I want you to know that we give you a curfew because we love you and want to give you freedom, but also make sure that you're safe.

In neither scenario should the father overlook Jill's disobedience. *This is not a matter of compromise.* This is about finding the sweet spot of disagreement without attacking. Dad and Jill love each other, but they must choose in this interaction to *speak* with love.

The conversation succeeds when we focus on the issue at hand (breaking curfew) instead of assigning motives (inconsiderate, disrespectful, controlling). We also see the danger of proceeding (usually in our anger) to deal with a problem before we have all the relevant information. Often a more subtle, loving approach will leave room for the guilty party to take ownership of what they have done without feeling they have to defend themselves. Attacking language prompts defensiveness and leads us away from solutions.

We need to be aware of the impact our social media "gotcha" culture is having on our ability to disagree. Online interactions encourage us to assume the worst about people we don't know very well. The line between substantive disagreement and personal insult is tragically blurred. "You probably didn't even go to school…I bet you live in your mother's basement…you're a fascist/Marxist." As we prepare our children to participate in this culture, we must show them the ability to disagree without personally attacking. We do not compromise on our convictions, but we do not attack. We speak with love.

Speaking with love may mean that we need to soften our tone and our words. We may need to express kindness intentionally. We may need to communicate more in general, sharing our thoughts and feelings with others and seeking to learn theirs. Sometimes we will need to calm down before speaking so that we do not damage those we love. It may be that we just need to clean up our language.

Sometimes little things matter a lot. Words change things. Words start wars—and end wars. Words start marriages—and end marriages. Words make us feel like we can't go on—and make us feel like we can.

We speak with love.

For Personal Introspection

- What cutting and hurtful words do I still remember someone saying to me? Why did they hurt me? Do I want to hurt and scar others with my words?
- Do I ever notice a difference in what I feel about others and how I speak to them?
- Is my speech harsh? How often do I have to apologize for things I've said? Is there a pattern here?
- What is my primary goal in my speaking—expressing myself, venting, insulting, or building others up?
- What strategies could I employ to disagree with my family without attacking them?

For Discussion

- Why do we want to let our guard down about our tongues? Why is this not a good idea? Is this true even with our families?
- Is there a difference between telling a negative truth about someone and insulting them?
- What kinds of statements build you up? Are there people whose encouragement means more to you than others? Why?
- What is the difference in discussing a behavior and attacking a person's character? Why do we respond differently when that line is crossed?

RULE 5

No Gossip Allowed

Other people are endlessly interesting to us. We want to hear their stories. We read news about what happens to them. We long to listen to their thoughts. We want to meet them and talk with them and live near them and love them. God has wired us for these connections. "It is not good that the man should be alone" (Gen 2:18).

Yet it is very easy (and common) for this people-fascination to take a dark turn. The most interesting things about people are often the most lurid, graphic, shameful, and disastrous. We are drawn to the drama. Did you hear what happened to so-and-so? We lean in to hear. We want to hear about the politician who does scandalous things—to discuss the televangelist with the drinking problem—to see the dark side of the rich dynastic families. We log on to social media not for information, but to see people squabble about the information. Perhaps bored by our own humdrum lives, we long for a window into other lives where something is happening that we can shake our heads at. So our fascination with people combines with our need to feel good about ourselves.

It gets closer to home. We start to talk about these things to others. Together we cluck our tongues and declare our superiority. It is a conspiracy of the condescending. *We* would never do that, say that, or be that. Can you believe what *they* did? We seek the approval and camaraderie of our friends at the cost of others' reputations. The content of such interactions is *never positive*. We do not lean in and whisper about others' *good* deeds. We spread negativity, criticism, damaging information, and sometimes things that are flat-out untrue. We color each other's view of a certain other person or group. We tear down for our own enjoyment.

In Christian homes, there is *no gossip allowed*.

WHAT IS GOSSIP?

Since gossip is an umbrella term for a lot of similar behaviors, some clarification is necessary. The essential idea here, blending together the various biblical expressions, is *saying bad things about other people to ruin their reputations or condemn them, especially when they are not present*.

The Bible uses the terms "gossip," "slander/slanderer," "speak evil," "speak against/blaspheme," "whisperer," "backbiter," "meddler," "reviling," and "busybody"—none of them positively. They are different dimensions of saying critical things about other people. It is distinct from saying things about people *directly to them*, which would represent a rebuke. Characteristic of gossip is that the subject of the gossip is absent. We are sharing their business with people who are not them.

The concept here is also motive-related. Not everything that has to do with others is gossip. Throughout the Bible, people report on others' actions. Sometimes we need to know what others are doing. Some information exchange is important here, especially if there is a physical or emotional danger. (I'm thinking particularly of kids being aware of unsafe people or telling parents about something that has happened to them). Occasionally we will need to discuss evil things that others have done (see Gal 6:1-2 and Matt 18:15-18). Yet the goal in these situations is to help, never to tear down.

The biblical witness is uniformly critical of gossip. "Do not speak evil against one another, brothers. The one who speaks against a brother or judges his brother, speaks evil against the law and judges the law" (James 4:11). Note the equation of speaking evil/slander with *judging*. We are taking a tone of superiority over others and presuming to condemn them. God warns against it; the judge's bench is already occupied.

But we are not only prohibited from gossiping about our Christian brothers and sisters. "Remind them…to speak evil of no one, to avoid quarreling, to be gentle, and to show perfect courtesy toward all people" (Titus 3:1, 2). The circle here is much wider—"no one" and "all people." This just should not be our practice.

The surgeon Philibert Joseph Roux summarized: "What is gossip? A verdict of 'guilty' pronounced in the absence of the accused, with closed doors, without defence or appeal, by an interested and prejudiced judge"[1]. A lot of the Bible terms emphasize this "closed doors" aspect of gossip as well. "Backbiting" (Rom 1:30, 2 Cor 12:20, NKJV), "whispering" (Rom 1:29, 2 Cor 12:20, NKJV), "meddling" (1 Pet 4:15), "busybodies" (2 Thess 3:11, 1 Tim 5:13), and "talebearer" (Prov 11:13, 18:8, 26:20, NKJV) all have elements of this discussion being inappropriate because the principal subject is absent.

Very often we justify our gossip by saying that "it's not gossip if it's true." I have two rebuttals. First, *not every true thing needs to be said*. Sometimes we are privileged to know information about others that would be damaging to them if it was told. Occasionally people (especially our children!) may ask us about matters that they don't need to know about which might damage their perceptions of others. To go ahead and share negative personal information like this when unnecessary requires some justification—even if it's true.

Second, *the fact that it's true doesn't mean my heart is pure*. When King Nebuchadnezzar sets up an enormous statue and orders the people to worship it, the Jews Shadrach, Meshach, and Abednego refrain. "Therefore at that time certain Chaldeans came forward and

---

1. https://www.inspiringquotes.us/author/4511-philibert-joseph-roux/page:3

maliciously accused the Jews…'These men, O king, pay no attention to you; they do not serve your gods or worship the golden image that you have set up'" (Dan 3:8, 12). Read through the accusation again. Is there anything untrue here? It is not the truth of the statement that makes it a "malicious accusation"; it is the sinister intent behind it. They are trying to harm.

So while there are certainly times when we must talk about others, I am suggesting a few things: *There is a significant problem here.* This is both a tendency we have and a practice repeatedly and roundly condemned in the Bible. *It's not fine just because it's true.* There are other factors to consider, such as whether others have a right to know something, whether I'm trying to help the person, and what the impact of my words will be. *Just because gossip is sometimes hard to distinguish from other speech doesn't mean it's all fine.* God is warning us against *something* here! *We cannot just say that this is our home and we'll talk how we want.* Not only will we damage others and disobey God, but we will also encourage our family to do so.

WHY DO WE GOSSIP?

What would motivate us to talk in this way about people? The Bible has several answers.

Laziness

In some of these texts, there is a strong connection drawn between idleness and gossip. Paul expresses to Timothy his concern about younger widows who "learn to be idlers, going about from house to house, and not only idlers, but also gossips and busybodies, saying what they should not. So I would have younger widows marry, bear children, manage their households, and give the adversary no occasion for slander" (1 Tim 5:13-14). I suspect that Paul had some experience with situations like this, where a widow being supported by the church at a young age (see 1 Tim 5:9) might not have enough to do. So, in her idleness, she floats from house to house, carrying news and gossip about the community. This idleness does not please God and this gossip sows discord within the church. Paul prescribes work for such young women.

It is not merely women. For some reason (speculations abound), many of the Christians in Thessalonica stop working. Paul sees this as a problem: "For we hear that some among you walk in idleness, not busy at work, but busybodies. Now such persons we command and encourage in the LORD Jesus Christ to do their work quietly and to earn their own living" (2 Thess 3:11-12). Instead of focusing on their own work, these idle people are "busybodies." This affects the community, which must now support them and withstand their destructive speech. Paul does not only advocate work; he wants them to "do their work *quietly*" (2 Thess 3:12, emphasis mine). The gossip needs to stop.

We worry about other people's business when we don't have enough of our own. In our laziness and inactivity, we seek a diversion—and other people are the greatest diversion there is. For modern Christians (and families), we must be aware of this tendency because our technologies connect us to a smorgasbord of information about other interesting people. When we are bored or stressed, gossip feels like a pleasant release.

Jealousy

Sometimes in our Bible study, we stumble onto an unanticipatedly rich vein of thought. This has been my experience in seeing the frequent connection between envy/jealousy and gossip/slander.

> But when the Jews saw the crowds, they were filled with jealousy and began to contradict what was spoken by Paul, reviling him (Acts 13:45).

So put away all malice and all deceit and hypocrisy and envy and all slander (1 Pet 2:1).

For I fear that perhaps when I come I may find you not as I wish, and that you may find me not as you wish—that perhaps there may be quarreling, jealousy, anger, hostility, slander, gossip, conceit, and disorder (2 Cor 12:20).

coveting, wickedness, deceit, sensuality, envy, slander, pride, foolishness. All these evil things come from within, and they defile a person (Mark 7:22-23).

he is puffed up with conceit and understands nothing. He has an unhealthy craving for controversy and for quarrels about words, which produce envy, dissension, slander, evil suspicions, and constant friction (1 Tim 6:4-5).

Any time we start to see the same words and ideas repeated in this many passages and different contexts, we should sit up and pay attention. There is a trend. Gossip produces envy (like when we love controversy and arguments, 1 Tim 6) and envy produces gossip (like when the Jews are jealous and "revile" Paul, Acts 13).

When we are jealous of others, we resent what they have. We feel they don't deserve their money, prestige, family, or talents. That feeling is rarely static. *We speak* out of our jealousy. This is where gossip can be a very subtle danger. We may not recognize that we are jealous. We feel we are just "stating facts" or "saying what we think about the situation." We fall back on our old standby, "well, it's true, isn't it?". Others also may not pick up on our jealousy.

What does jealous gossip sound like? "You know, I know Bob has a lot of money, but he just wastes it on fancy stuff. When we went to his house, did you see how many TVs he has? And why does he need a house that big?" "She just prances around because she wants everybody to see how beautiful she is." "He thinks he's hot stuff, but his kids are out of control." "He's a terrible boss! I don't know what they were thinking by promoting him! Everybody hates him!" When we look a little deeper beneath the surface of comments like these, we see that the real source of the resentment we are expressing is jealousy. We want the money they have; we seek their respect; we deserve that job; we want to one-up them. This deeper thinking helps us to see gossip for the sinister evil that it is. A heart that can only look at others' blessings with jealousy and bitterness is in desperate need of reform. Even sadder is the possibility that my family's opinions of others would be colored by my own pettiness.

When we are jealous, our goal in speaking is to ruin the reputation of others and win people over to our poor estimation of them. In what universe is this Christian? This is the reason it doesn't really matter whether gossip is technically true; no amount of truth will redeem this corrupt motive.

Hurt

When people hurt us (emotionally), we usually do not suffer in silence. We tell others about it. "But now you must put them all away: anger, wrath, malice, slander, and obscene talk from your mouth" (Col 3:8). These are manifestations of our anger that Paul says are unproductive in the long-term. Among them is "slander"— the rush to tell uninvolved people about the horrible way in which someone has hurt us. Paul contrasts these reactions with forgiveness (see Col 3:12-13 and Eph 4:31-32). His point is that *gossip is a way we attempt to get revenge on those who have wounded us*. I may not be able to hurt you in precisely the same way you hurt me, but I can run you down to other people! In this context, again, the facts are less important than our motives. Whether we are reporting what happened or telling others what we "really think" about someone, it remains an act of revenge. We speak out of our hurt.

Similarly, Peter gives us an order: "Do not repay evil for evil or reviling for reviling, but on the contrary, bless, for to this you were called, that you may obtain a blessing" (1 Pet 3:9). Even when others are speaking evil of us, our "reviling" of them is not justified. We are called to something higher.

But does this mean we can never tell anyone about our pain? Is any effort to explain our past gossip by definition? My answer to both questions is no. NT authors do not tell us to ignore our pain and sublimate our feelings; they tell us to *deal with our problems directly and quickly.* Jesus says this repeatedly (Matt 5:23-24, 18:15). Paul tells us to "not let the sun go down on our anger" (Eph 4:26), meaning that we don't delay in reconciling with people who have wounded us. We must acknowledge the danger our pain and anger hold for our relationships and for our own hearts. We must go fix the problem, as soon as possible. *This is entirely different from gossip, which involves unrelated parties and gets us no closer to solutions.*

The other consideration here is *the need to be honest about our motives.* Are we saying these words or acting in this way in an effort to get revenge? What am I thinking? What is my goal?

Fun

It's best to just acknowledge this: gossip is entertaining and fun. "The words of a whisperer are like delicious morsels; they go down into the inner parts of the body" (Prov 18:8). "Delicious morsels" highlights the pleasure we get from talking in a derogatory way about others. Even today we call it "juicy" gossip. We learn things about people and enjoy the shattering of their facades. We get to act shocked, cover our mouths in surprise, and exclaim, "No!". It is all great fun.

Part of the appeal is that we get to judge others. We get to feel like we are better than they are. Did you hear what they did? I never…I would never…That's unbelievable!

Part of the appeal is that it draws us just a little bit closer to the people we are gossiping with. A bond is formed. When we feel insecure and unaccepted by a group, telling unflattering things about others pulls us together. Now we belong. Now it's us against them. We have made friends—at least superficially. We have something to offer—something interesting to say—something to make others appreciate us.

The reinforcement of that superiority is part of what makes gossip so poisonous in a family. When we teach one another that gossip is fun and rewarding, it becomes a habit that is hard to break. When we feel insecure, hurt, or bored, we pull out our harsh judgments of others and feel the comfort of criticizing. We are teaching one another a habit that is very often connected with evil or dubious motives.

WHY IS GOSSIP A PROBLEM?

Gossip hurts people.

It should not surprise us that when we talk about others in order to tear them down, ruin their reputation, and turn others against them, we achieve our goal. "A dishonest man spreads strife, and a whisperer separates close friends" (Prov 16:28). When we whisper about others, we "(separate) close friends." When we do this, we harm relationships. And when we knock Humpty Dumpty down, it's almost impossible to put him back together again.

When someone says, "Did you hear what Elizabeth said about you?", suddenly my relationship with Elizabeth is harmed. I know that she has been talking about me with someone else in a negative way, which hurts me. Then I know that this person telling me is willing to gossip about me, then come and gossip with me about Elizabeth. I am unclear as to what was actually said—especially because the truth in such situations is extremely difficult to ascertain—but the damage is done regardless. What were the motives? What was the context? I may never know, but I know that I have been wounded. I now have to choose whether to confront Elizabeth about what she has said, swallow my hurt and try to get over it, or gossip about her to others. Gossip hurts people.

"The north wind brings forth rain, and a backbiting tongue, angry looks" (Prov 25:23). Want to make someone angry? Speak harshly about them without giving them a chance to defend themselves.

"For lack of wood the fire goes out, and where there is no whisperer, quarreling ceases. As charcoal to hot embers and wood to fire, so is a quarrelsome man for kindling strife" (Prov 26:20-21). Want to cause friction and drama in your relationships? Whisper about people when they're not around.

It surprises me how frequently I encounter Christians who seek to justify gossip. No matter how many Bible passages prohibit it or how much experience warns against it, we defend our practice. We push back about definitions and severity. So perhaps it would help us to simply declare that *gossip is not a victimless crime*. It hurts people. We may think others will never know, but they often do. Yet even when they do not, *we* are hurt by the thoughts and motives we have harbored.

Gossip destroys trust.

We will discover things about people that are not flattering. This is particularly true of Christians, who are taught to "confess your sins to one another and pray for one another, that you may be healed" (James 5:16). We will know each other's business—even the bad stuff. Can we be trusted not to gossip?

"Whoever goes about slandering reveals secrets; therefore do not associate with a simple babbler" (Prov 20:19). We all know people like this who cannot be trusted with sensitive information. Maybe it's that they talk too much or maybe that they don't have discretion. We learn very quickly that they are unworthy of our confidences. The vital question is *whether we are that sort of people*. Gossip proves that we are.

"Whoever covers an offense seeks love, but he who repeats a matter separates close friends" (Prov 17:9). When we observe an "offense," whether personally or indirectly, we can either "cover" it or tell others about it. Covering a sin or problem is a way we help others move forward and overcome; it is how we "(seek) love." If we will only tell others about it, we are unworthy of others' trust.

"Whoever goes about slandering reveals secrets, but he who is trustworthy in spirit keeps a thing covered" (Prov 11:13). Gossip and trustworthiness are opposites.

I wonder, too, whether this is not what Peter means when he speaks about the suffering of gossipers. "But let none of you suffer as a murderer or a thief or an evildoer or as a meddler" (1 Pet 4:15). There is nobility in suffering for Jesus, but there is no virtue in bringing pain on ourselves. Somehow being a "meddler" brings suffering; is it possible the suffering is the relational damage we have caused with our meddling?

CREATING AN ANTI-GOSSIP HOME

How can we do better? How do we make this Bible teaching a house rule?

Start with self.

Any change in our homes must begin with introspection rather than criticism. A large part of the battle here is simply awareness. When we talk about others, we need the conscious thought that we do not want to cross the line into gossip, negativity, backbiting, or slander. It will also help us to monitor what is happening in our hearts as we talk. I have found these questions helpful:

What are the facts? Am I assuming someone else's motives? What do I know for certain? What part of this is my perception? Am I accusing them of something? We easily confuse our impression of a situation with the facts. What part of what I am about to say is my own opinion?

Does this need to be said? This is about being audience-aware. Is this information relevant to my kids or my wife? The fact that I know something doesn't mean I need to say it. I belong to Jesus. All my words are under his control. All my words will judge me (Matt 12:36-37). *All my words must be scanned to ensure that I am not speaking evil.* I may think it; it may be true; is it *necessary*?

What are my motives? Why do I want to say this? Am I bored? Jealous? Do I want to get someone on my side? Am I seeking validation? I have discovered that when I feel awkward in social situations, I talk too much. I sometimes reveal things I did not intend and say things I don't really mean. My desire to save face in front of people—or to get them to like me—cannot be allowed to lead me to wrong others.

Ask "hold on a second" questions.

When we find ourselves in a gossip situation in our home, we can gently push back on each other by asking questions. These are questions that, instead of going with the flow of criticizing others, reframe the discussion. They can be requests for clarification: "Are you sure she said that?" or "I have a hard time believing that about him" or "Is that what they said or just what you heard?". They can be questions to turn down the emotional temperature of the gossiper: "Why does that make you so angry?" or "What do you think they're thinking when they say that?". Or they can be questions to stop things in their tracks, such as "Haven't you ever done something like that?". The goal here is to disrupt the gossip situation before it progresses to slander.

Push back with understanding.

When we hear our kids or spouses begin to gossip, we can take responsibility for defending the accused in their absence. From time to time my kids would report about some out-of-control classmate, especially when they were hit by his emotional shrapnel. Upon further investigation, we would often discover that these kids had very rocky home lives, emotional issues, or were just very lonely. When we advised our kids, we tried to explain the need to understand their hard background and have compassion. This doesn't justify their misbehavior, but it helps soften us and quiets our anger. Efforts to understand others are not only a part of Christian compassion, they are also a way we break the self-centeredness of gossip situations.

To push back successfully, we can ask questions. Why would someone do something like that? What are they thinking? What are they afraid of? Would I respond the way they did in that situation? If we are going to talk about others, let's do it with kindness and understanding.

Find something to compliment.

A dear Christian sister told me about her husband's strategy for combating gossip among his friends. When a group was gathered around him skewering a mutual acquaintance in absentia, he would wait calmly, not participating in the conversation. Then he would quietly say, "You know, when you think about it, he's really a pretty good guy." The tone of the talk would swiftly turn to praising the good.

Compliments are less about the specific content than about changing the tone. Even when we are frustrated with other people—even when they have hurt us—they are not all bad. There are things to admire in everyone; isn't that a better topic of conversation than all the things to despise?

Refuse to participate.

When we are outside a family-only setting, it can be hard to control gossip. When with non-Christians, they may not understand our reasoning in why we don't talk about people this way (or just think it's silly). The best course may be to simply not join in others' criticisms. When there is no friendly ear, most gossip dies out on its own.

A culture of gossip in our homes—rather than a culture of kind speech—will color our family's opinions of every person they encounter. There is a danger of overexposing our children to information so that they know so much about others that all they can see is their flaws. There is an opposing danger of oversheltering our kids so that they don't think anyone around them is real because they don't know enough about them. We should pray for discretion and wisdom. *But the answer is not to just say what we feel like since it's our home.*

Other people are endlessly fascinating to us, but fixating on their negative qualities can hurt them and us. *No gossip allowed.*

For Personal Introspection

- In what ways do other people interest me? Does this ever take a sinister turn?
- What was the climate about gossip in my raising? Is my home like that now?
- How do I respond when I am hurt? Am I ever tempted to speak evil of people who have done me wrong?
- What one change could I make to avoid being a party to gossip?

For Discussion

- How have we seen gossip cause problems? How have we been affected by others gossiping about us?
- Is gossip acceptable if it's true? In what circumstances might it be OK to share negative things about others?
- What should we do if someone close to us has a problem with gossip? How could we gently and kindly help the situation?
- How will we know when everyday discussion crosses the line into something problematic?

RULE

6

We Take Responsibility

The 2017 U.S. Open was not a great experience for Italian tennis player Fabio Fognini. During a match, he had three temper tantrums, called the umpire some awful names, lost, and was later fined $24,000 for his behavior[1]. He posted this apology on Twitter: "I would first apologize to you fans and the referee about what happened today. It's just been a very bad day, but this does not forgive the behavior in the match! Although I'm a hothead (and though in my opinion having been right in most circumstances), I made a mistake. Then at the end of the day it's only a game of tennis."[2]

I would encourage a re-reading of this "apology." He's having a bad day. He's a hothead. And he's right about most of the bad calls. But he made a mistake. But it's only tennis.

This follows a pattern of a lot of "apologies," especially in the sports world. We are aware that people are mad, so we know we should say something. But we also want to tell our own side of the story! And we still feel like we're right to feel the way we do. So we give this kind of schizophrenic excuse. I'm sorry *that you got offended.*

---

1. https://www.foxsports.com.au/tennis/us-open/tennis-bad-boy-fabio-fognini-booted-from-us-open-after-disgusting-slur-directed-at-female-umpire/news-story/e93d556f2bf963cc8ffdf4970382e28c
2. https://twitter.com/fabiofogna/status/903193499511742464/photo/1

I'm sorry *that you took it that way*. I'm sorry, *but it's only tennis*. (In his defense, Fognini later offered a fuller apology. He has also thrown further tantrums and received more fines since this incident[3][4][5].)

Home is the place where we learn that there are areas that are uniquely our responsibility. It's where we practice doing our own jobs, taking care of ourselves, learning the impact of our actions, and, yes, taking ownership when we mess up. There are some things no one else can do for us. To be healthy, productive workers and good citizens—from the factory floor to the freeway to the tennis court—we must develop this sense of what is ours and what is not.

We take responsibility.

I AM RESPONSIBLE FOR MY WORK

Paul frames the issue of responsibility in Christian terms by describing our work as something we *bear*.

> Brothers, if anyone is caught in any transgression, you who are spiritual should restore him in a spirit of gentleness. Keep watch on yourself, lest you too be tempted. Bear one another's burdens, and so fulfill the law of Christ. For if anyone thinks he is something, when he is nothing, he deceives himself. But let each one test his own work, and then his reason to boast will be in himself alone and not in his neighbor. For each will have to bear his own load (Gal 6:2-5).

---

3. https://metro.co.uk/2019/07/08/fabio-fognini-fined-yelling-bomb-explode-wimbledon-10134794/

4. https://www.reuters.com/lifestyle/sports/fognini-defaulted-verbal-abuse-barcelona-open-2021-04-21/

5. https://www.tennisworldusa.org/tennis/news/Tennis_Interviews/71286/fabio-fognini-i-got-fined-by-the-italian-open/

As fellow-disciples, we help each other when we have overwhelming needs. Paul has in mind a situation in which someone is caught up in sin (Gal 6:1) and needs our help dealing with the problem. He likens these circumstances to someone carrying a load that has become overwhelming, so we carry it for them for a while. In this way we "bear one another's burdens, and so fulfill the law of Christ." We are most like Jesus when we are helping meet other's needs.

But he does not stop there. There is a danger that when we help others with their needs, we will start to think too much of ourselves. We need to consider that we are not better than others who are struggling (Gal 6:1); our time of struggle will come too. Paul is concerned that we will think we are more than we are (Gal 6:3). His solution is that "each one test his own work, and then his reason to boast will be in himself alone and not in his neighbor." We will not ride the coattails of others' work. We will not look better because others look worse. Instead, *we each have our own work.* "For each will have to bear his own load."

There are things that I can only do for myself. They are my responsibility. They are my work. For example, only I can obey God for me. You can't do that. No matter how much we would like to, we cannot do the right thing in place of our children. One of the great blessings and challenges of family life is learning how to blend our lives together while preserving the fact that each of us has our own unique work and responsibilities.

In the last rule we discussed the Thessalonian Christians, who had stopped working to provide for themselves. Paul tells them "to aspire to live quietly, and to mind your own affairs, and to work with your hands, as we instructed you, so that you may walk properly before outsiders and be dependent on no one" (1 Thess 4:11-12). Each of us has a sphere of responsibility ("your own affairs") and capability ("work with your hands") that God expects us to use so that we meet our own physical needs ("be dependent on no one"). I am responsible for my work.

When I fail to do my own work, I neglect God's purpose for me. He has given each person a special blend of skills and personality, which he wants us to use to work—including both "paying" work and work that is not for an employer.

But when I fail to do my own work, I also become a burden on others. Paul wants Christians to "be dependent on no one" (1 Thess 4:12) not because he is a rugged American individualist, but because this is an abuse of others' generosity. He wants Christians to take care of their own families—including widows in their families—so that "the church not be burdened, so that it may care for those who are truly widows" (1 Tim 5:16). When I falter in my responsibilities, my needs spill over onto others. There is a difference in tragedy or injury making me needy and idleness making me dependent. *It is not loving to force others to care for me because I refuse to take responsibility.*

In fact, Paul stresses that this is part of the transformation God works in new Christians. "Let the thief no longer steal, but rather let him labor, doing honest work with his own hands, so that he may have something to share with anyone in need" (Eph 4:28). Notice the shift from taking to giving. Instead of stealing, we work. Yet our work is not just for our own needs, but also to "have something to share with anyone in need." This is God's plan for our "extra." The difference between relying on others to take care of us and choosing to take care of others is night and day. *By taking responsibility for my work, I can be free to help those who are truly needy.*

I hope you have noticed the different uses I have made of the idea of "my work." My work involves meeting my own *physical* needs. I may receive things from others—I may be given gifts or help—but that does not change my fundamental responsibility to do my own work. There is also *spiritual* work that is my duty. I have obligations to God to obey and serve him. There are life-changes no one can make for me. My moral decisions are my call. Others can encourage me, warn me, or be ambivalent, but no one can do these things for me. My parents cannot do this for me, nor can my spouse. It is my work.

For many of us, our work includes some measure of leadership. I am a husband and a father. With those roles comes the responsibility to care for my wife, protect and provide for her, consider her needs, and manage our relationship. As a father, I carry the responsibility to provide for and protect my children, teach them about Jesus and about life, discipline them, and help them grow. No one can do these things for me. Others might help. Others might even be forced to step into some of those roles if I fall down on the job. Yet I am responsible.

The concept we are establishing here is that each person has *spheres* in which they hold certain roles and obligations. Christian homes are places where we are willing to accept the responsibilities that come with these roles. This kind of teaching and thinking cannot start too early, especially when we deal with our children. At a very early age, children can learn that they have a set of things that are *theirs*. The exact thing can vary: toys, books, rooms, clothes, etc. The point is that *with the blessing of possession comes the need to take responsibility for the possession.* I need to keep my place clean, not destroy my books, or put my toys where they go. Perhaps there is a small chore or set of rules that a young child has so he or she can learn to do the work of managing their sphere. The goal here is never so that we will have more help around the house (in my experience, involving kids in cleaning makes *more* work!), but to teach that "each one bears his own load." As children grow and mature, those responsibilities increase. A child learns to care for a pet, keep the bathroom clean, or do laundry. A child learns that schoolwork is her "job," just like preaching is my job. Teenagers grow to manage money, keep a car clean, pay bills, and show up at work on time. We learn the satisfaction of doing a job very well. Privileges are hinged on performing responsibilities well.

In time, of course, this awareness of personal responsibility extends into the spiritual realm. Having been trained to think of what they need to do, manage, and answer for, our kids learn that they stand on their own before God. They have their own set of obligations to him—and their own imperfect record in that relationship. They begin to bear their own load.

Christian homes stress—by teaching, example, and practice—that I am responsible for my work.

I AM RESPONSIBLE FOR MY ACTIONS

How does God want his people to live? Paul tells us specifically: "For this is the will of God, your sanctification: that you abstain from sexual immorality; that each one of you know how to control his own body in holiness and honor, not in the passion of lust like the Gentiles who do not know God" (1 Thess 4:3-5). God's will is that we be *holy*. Here that contains the dimension of sexual purity and self-control. Specifically he wants "that each one of you know how to control his own body in holiness and honor." "Each one of you" is important here because it stresses personal responsibility; I cannot control your body but I must control my own. When I fail to control my own body, I alone am responsible for the things that I have done. If I live in the passion of lust like godless people, then I will have to answer to God for rebelling against his will. I am responsible for my actions—and no one else.

That doesn't mean that my actions *affect* only me! Sexual sin particularly has a way of doing damage far out of proportion to the act itself. Paul warns that we can "transgress and wrong (our) brother in this matter" (1 Thess 4:6). When I am a part of my family, my actions affect everyone in my family. Often my actions affect my co-workers, my fellow students, my church family, and sometimes my neighbors, teammates, or fellow citizens. The consequences can ripple far beyond myself, but I am responsible for them.

Yet Paul's words here also teach us the limits of our responsibility. If I am responsible for my actions, then that means that *there is never a situation where the temptation is too strong, the person is too beautiful or handsome, or it is someone else's fault.* I always have a choice in how I act. For example, as a Christian man I attempt to remain pure in my thinking regarding women, even being careful how I look at them (Matt 5:27-28). Yet I am not responsible for the clothes that women wear or fail to wear. I am responsible for my own eyes, thoughts, and actions. I certainly could wish that women would dress appropriately—and I encourage Christian women to dress appropriately—but I must control myself no matter what. Similarly, Christian women cannot control what men do, say, or think about them sexually. That is not their responsibility. But they can control what they wear, how they present themselves, and what they show the world about who they are. *I am responsible for my own actions—and only my own.*

Anger fits here too. Jesus teaches us, "You have heard that it was said to those of old, 'You shall not murder; and whoever murders will be liable to judgment.' But I say to you that everyone who is angry with his brother will be liable to judgment; whoever insults his brother will be liable to the council; and whoever says 'You fool!' will be liable to the hell of fire" (Matt 5:21-22). Has anyone ever made you angry? We have all had that experience. Anger in itself is not wrong; Jesus' statement here focuses on what we *do* with that anger (insulting and condemning our brother). He warns that even though these are not murder, they are in the same category and come from the same heart.

But did you notice the responsibility-shifting in the question? "Has anyone ever made you angry?" is a question that blames others for our own choices. I'm mad, but it's *their* fault. We must be aware of the subtlety with which we (and our spouses and children) seek to avoid responsibility for our own actions. If I am responsible for my own actions, then I am not responsible for how others treat me. They may "make me mad," meaning that I have a certain emotional response to their actions. *But my response is my responsibility.*

In a home, this gets very practical very quickly. One child keeps needling another, and the second child lashes out. How can we establish parental justice? *Responsibility for our own actions* is a principle that will guide us. Being mad doesn't mean our actions are OK. Others' disobedience doesn't justify my own.

A wife, frustrated with her husband, says something to push his emotional buttons. He rants and raves and says his own ugly things. *Responsibility for our own actions* will guide us to cleaning up the mess, offering appropriate apologies, and preventing similar blowups in the future.

We will have more to say about anger later in this book, but here I will simply state that *I am responsible for what I do when I am angry*—my words, my treatment of others, my bitterness, and my raising of my voice. That means that *there is never a situation where the temptation is too strong, the person is too infuriating or annoying, or the insult is too harsh*, so that I just must lash out.

Christian homes must teach and live by this mindset. I am responsible for my body and my anger. I am responsible for my words—good or bad. I am responsible for my money. I am responsible for my free time. There will be temptations to sin in each of these areas. There will be people who will whisper that we should do something inappropriate or immoral. Yet the choice is always mine. I am responsible for my actions.

In Christian homes, we can teach this principle by stressing *expectations* for each other's actions. Husbands and wives expect certain things from each other—and the more clearly that those expectations are stated, the better. How do we address each other? What kinds of things are off-limits? We don't call each other names (that's a rule for adults too) or push each other. In our home, we try to teach the expectation that we respect each other's "no"—laying the groundwork for respecting others' boundaries (and expecting them to respect ours). Our thinking is that what begins now—the expectation that you stop tickling me when I tell you, get out of my room when I ask, or quit asking me repeatedly what I have answered—will form expectations for *later* situations (like saying no to a pushy boyfriend, friends inviting us to do something bad, or our own impulses). As kids mature, we expect kindness toward others who are different from us. We expect our family to remember the rules of the family even when our kids are out with their friends. We expect self-discipline while in the classroom.

When those clear expectations are then violated, there is no question as to who is at fault. In the ensuing discussion about discipline and remedy, this house rule becomes vital. Parents can show understanding for the fact that the situation may have been unforeseen or difficult to navigate. We are careful and patient. But we can still insist that our children take responsibility for their own choices.

I AM RESPONSIBLE FOR MY MESSES

Here we return to Mr. Fognini. Sometimes we fail. Sometimes we fail in ways that are spectacularly public, such as when we lose our cool during a major tennis match. Home is where we learn the essential Christian practice of owning—and beginning to clean up—our messes.

King David is a powerful example in this. He spirals out of control after seeing Bathsheba bathing, pursuing her despite them both being married, committing adultery with her, then scheming to have her husband killed. It is a dark chapter. From our vantage, it is easy to see whose fault all this is (and Scripture has no word of censure for Bathsheba, Uriah, Nathan, or any other character in the story). *What do we do when we mess up?* Through the prophet Nathan's intervention, David comes to terms with his sin and pens this poignant psalm:

> Have mercy on me, O God, according to your steadfast love; according to your abundant mercy blot out my transgressions. Wash me thoroughly from my iniquity, and cleanse me from my sin! For I know my transgressions, and my sin is ever before me. Against you, you only, have I sinned and done what is evil in your sight, so that you may be justified in your words and blameless in your judgment. Behold, I was brought forth in iniquity, and in sin did my mother conceive me. Behold, you delight in truth in the inward being, and you teach me wisdom in the secret heart. Purge me with hyssop, and I shall be clean; wash me, and I shall be whiter than snow. Let me hear joy and gladness; let the bones that you have broken rejoice. Hide your face from my sins, and blot out all my iniquities. Create in me a clean heart, O God, and renew a right spirit within me (Psalm 51:1-10).

David offers no excuses for his sin. He does not say, "I'm sorry, God, but Bathsheba was so hot!" or "She shouldn't have been bathing where I could see her!" or "Why did you make me with this sexual desire?". The problem here is not with anyone else. Nor does David minimize what he has done, as if it is merely "an error in judgment" or "a mistake" or some nonsense about how "we're all human." In this psalm, David is simply exploring, with new depth, the words that he spoke upon first realizing his tremendous error: "I have sinned against the LORD" (2 Sam 12:13). Say those words slowly, and with feeling, and you will sense their power. There is transformative humility in taking responsibility for our messes.

And so David is moved to pray. He is deeply in need of God's mercy, which he does not deserve. He knows the stain of his evil ("my sin is ever before me") and feels that it tarnishes his whole life ("I was brought forth in iniquity"). He desperately hungers to be clean again, innocent again, honest again. *Only when he takes responsibility for his mess does David connect to God and begin to heal.* This does not excuse David's sin; there is no excuse for the harm he has done. This does not remove the consequences of David's sin in his own reign and the lives of others; Bathsheba's husband will not come back to life. But God can forgive and the story can continue.

Daniel also shows us that this can also involve taking responsibility for *our part in a larger mess*. Daniel lives most of his life in Babylon because Judah has been conquered, decimated, and taken captive for their sin.

> Then I turned my face to the LORD God, seeking him by prayer and pleas for mercy with fasting and sackcloth and ashes. I prayed to the LORD my God and made confession, saying, 'O LORD, the great and awesome God, who keeps covenant and steadfast love with those who love him and keep his commandments, we have sinned and done wrong and acted wickedly and rebelled, turning aside from your commandments and rules. We have not listened to your servants the prophets, who spoke in your name to our kings, our princes, and our fathers, and to all the people of the land. To you, O LORD, belongs righteousness, but to us open shame. (Dan 9:3-7)

Daniel identifies himself as a part of Judah's disobedience. *We* have sinned. *We* have not listened. *We* deserve open shame. By all accounts, Daniel is a man of exemplary character, yet he takes responsibility for his part in what has happened to the nation. He does not distance himself from the other Jews; these are his people! Nor does he blame God for unfairness for punishing him for the sins of his fathers (as some of his countrymen do, Ezek 18:1-3, Jer 31:29-30). God is right. We are wrong.

Rule 6: We Take Responsibility

The Bible rings with the words of godly people taking such responsibility for their messes. "I have sinned." "I have done very foolishly." "Pray for me to the LORD." *We must learn this.*

There are some obstacles. *Our world is strongly resistant to taking responsibility for our own messes.* "I'm sorry you took it that way" or "I'm sorry if anyone was offended" actually put the blame *on the other person*! I remember watching a talk show (specific details have escaped my memory) in which a husband who cheated on his wife berated her: I said I was sorry! What more do you want from me? How long are you going to wait to forgive me? *Taking responsibility means that we accept that our mess may have permanently changed everything—and it is our fault.* My wife may not trust me again when I betray her. That's not her fault. I may have trouble getting a job if I have been dishonest with my boss. That's not a problem with the company; it's my fault. In a society that values victimhood, Christian homes must be countercultural.

We will struggle with this kind of accountability if we *tend to offer excuses and justifications*. I was under a lot of stress. I'm just a hothead. That's the way I was raised. It's only tennis.

We will struggle with this if we *tend to blame others*. I had a rough home life. The people made me do it. If they hadn't provoked me, I wouldn't have had to punch them. I know it was wrong, but you had it coming.

We will struggle with this if we *tend to think that we are right because our intent was good*. King Saul had a really good reason for disobeying God (1 Sam 15); it didn't fly. Sometimes we make mistakes unwittingly. That is sad and hard to swallow. But messes are still messes and sin is still sin.

This attitude of humility, admission, and apology should be learned young, at home. In Christian homes, some phrases should be in regular use: I didn't know that. I made a mistake. I shouldn't have said/done that. You're right. Can you forgive me? I messed up.

When we break the rules, we admit it. *That starts with parents.* Parental authority is not permission to act as an infallible tyrant. It is entirely appropriate for parents to humble themselves before their children and admit their mistakes. My kids need to hear when I am reevaluating my actions and discover that I haven't been what I should be. They need to hear that I am sorry for yelling or getting too angry. They need to hear that I regret a decision I made. They need to hear that I should not have spoken to their mother that way, spent money that way, or dealt with that person that way. By owning their messes, parents teach their children that *even grown-ups must be thinking about right and wrong.* Parents teach children *the vocabulary of humility.* Parents teach children that *love sometimes says I'm sorry.* These moments are tone-setters in our homes; we cannot pass up an opportunity to own our mess.

When spouses argue and hurt one another, taking responsibility means dropping our offensive posture (she's the one at fault) and our defensive posture (I haven't done anything wrong) to ask: *How am I contributing to this problem?* What is my role in this mess? I have found that a great way to break marital gridlock is to admit and sincerely apologize for my own part in conflict and mistakes. It is hard to fight with a spouse who is agreeing with you—and it usually leads to reciprocation in which our mate apologizes for their own part.

This also affects the way we indulge our children's excuses. We all love our kids and would prefer not to punish them. We naturally take their side in a dispute with a friend or teacher. But when we continue to excuse behavior—especially when it creates a problem—we are undermining a healthy sense of responsibility for mistakes. It is essential that we balance understanding our kids' perspective and reasoning with consistent reminders of what is within their sphere of control and accountability.

THE RESPONSIBILITY CONVERSATION

Many marriages struggle because the division of responsibilities and labor is understood rather than agreed upon. A husband enters marriage with the assumption that his wife will cook and clean—possibly because that is what he saw his mother do—while the wife is unaware of these expectations. A wife believes that her husband is going to attend to the yard, the bills, or even just pick up his laundry, yet soon discovers that he has no intention of doing any of these things. Conflict often results from these preconceptions.

A high-level conversation is needed here. Without any anger or resentment, we must work out who will do what in the family. *All responsibilities are assigned by agreement.* Someone must express a willingness to take the trash out, to do dishes, or to manage money. Agreement is essential here because it means we are no longer judging each other by unspoken expectations. We then understand that our failure to fulfill our commitment will disappoint and frustrate our spouse, who is counting on us to take care of it. When I agree to be in charge of the trash, we all know whose fault it is when the house begins to stink. Alongside taking responsibility comes the expectation that I will consistently meet my obligation and be accountable to others for that. It may be that future conversations are needed to add new chores and tasks, always by consent, to our set of responsibilities. Similar conversations can help children understand their roles and the expectations of them. What I cannot stress enough, though, is that *talking in terms of responsibility will help us see the importance of pulling our own weight, admitting when we have failed, and building a basic sense of self-worth.*

Taking responsibility starts at home and radiates outward. Without it, we show up to work and resent being asked to do our jobs. We attend local churches and expect others to serve us. We leech off others. We frustrate others. We sow discord in extended families. And then, when the problem grows more acute, we insist that it's not *our* fault!

But responsible homes produce responsible workers, church members, and friends. They make our society a better place in which to live. And when we fail to do what we should, those from responsible homes spread the healthy humility of owning our mistakes.

We take responsibility.

For Personal Introspection

- What spheres of responsibility does my "work" include? In what areas of my work do I struggle taking responsibility? Why might that be?
- The author states that when we fail to take responsibility, we become a burden to others. Have I ever done this? Have others done this to me?
- When was the last time I admitted my own sin?
- What excuses and rationalizations do I tend to offer for my messes?

For Discussion

- What do you think of Fabio Fognini's apology? How might it be improved? Why is the wording of our apologies so important?
- What is the difference between others *influencing* our actions and others being *responsible* for our actions?
- The author cites Daniel as an example of someone who admitted his role in a national failure. Is it appropriate to take responsibility for a group failure? Where might this be necessary (church, nation, city, generational family)? Why might this be healthy? Why might it be hard?
- Why is it hard to take responsibility for our mistakes in family situations?

RULE 7

We Deal with Our Problems

As the youngest of three brothers, I grew up hating confrontation. In a home with several big personalities, I learned quickly that it's easier to just let them have their way. I didn't want to fight all the time—especially because, being the smallest, I lost a lot of those fights. So I learned to swallow my feelings and opinions and keep the peace, even when I had a problem.

But when I became an adult, I discovered how tremendously unhealthy and unsustainable avoiding conflict is. When I mute my feelings and concerns now, my family suffers. People take advantage of us. Losing money doesn't just affect me; it also takes it out of the pockets of my wife and kids. And the need to iron out differences in my extended family, my nuclear family, and my church family just keeps coming up. You can only avoid it so many times before the problems escalate and a new approach is needed.

I suspect that there are not many people who *do* enjoy confrontation. Some people excel at arguing, but true hostility is unpleasant to most of us. Yet there is a powerful biblical principle that addresses this reluctance. *God's people deal with their problems with others.*

When God gave people his law through Moses, he warned them:

Rule 7: We Deal with Our Problems

> You shall not hate your brother in your heart, but you shall reason frankly with your neighbor, lest you incur sin because of him. You shall not take vengeance or bear a grudge against the sons of your own people, but you shall love your neighbor as yourself; I am the LORD (Lev 19:17-18).

The context here is about interpersonal wrongs and misconduct in court settings. God wants his people not to just "hate your brother in your heart," but to plainly express whatever frustrations or concerns we have with them. We are to "reason frankly with (our) neighbor". Other versions render this as "rebuke your neighbor frankly" (NIV) or "don't secretly hate your brother. If you have something against him, get it out in the open" (The Message).

The caution here is that we must not let hate fester. Get it out. Talk it out. Say what needs to be said. Do what needs to be done. Deal with your problems.

And I am suggesting that this is a process that will have great power when learned and practiced at home.

WHY DO WE DEAL WITH OUR PROBLEMS?

Since confrontation is so unpleasant, it will help us to see the benefits it brings. We do not deal with our problems because we are inflexible and everyone else needs to change to accommodate us. Nor are we motivated by a desire to have everything in our lives be constantly perfect. So why should we "get it out in the open"?

To Maintain Healthy Relationships

We see a hint of this in the text we have already noticed. "You shall not hate your brother in your heart" (Lev 19:17). Someone we know has done something to us that has produced hate in our hearts and we simply choose to hold it in. We do not, the text implies, "reason frankly" with him. We just stew. We keep brooding over the slight or offense. We keep telling ourselves how right we are. We tell sympathetic others how unfair the other person is. The problem grows so far out of proportion that we feel it is worth sacrificing our relationship and dedicating our lives to our victimhood.

This is not healthy—for us or them. Something is broken here.

Very often we become convinced that it is the other person's fault that the relationship has grown sour. That may be true. But notice that the text here has *no concern whatsoever for what he has done to me.* "You shall not hate your brother in your heart, but you shall reason frankly with your neighbor, lest you incur sin because of him" (Lev 19:17). God is telling me not to hold hate in *my* heart. If I do, their evil becomes my evil. Their sin becomes my sin. I have been overcome by evil instead of overcoming evil with good (Rom 12:21).

This is also what Paul is after with his teaching on anger. "Be angry and do not sin; do not let the sun go down on your anger, and give no opportunity to the devil" (Eph 4:26-27). Recognizing that anger is a dangerous emotion that puts us at risk (both physically and spiritually), Paul warns us not to allow it to linger. If relationships are characterized by anger, they are unhealthy. He is not saying that we can simply rant and rave until we don't feel angry anymore; he is telling us that we must proactively resolve our anger—without sin—or else we give Satan an "opportunity." Paul adds particular urgency to the instruction by telling us to "not let the sun go down on your anger." We cannot live with unresolved anger in our hearts; it will not just go away. Holding hate within us will corrupt us and grow to consume us. *We deal with our problems.*

Jesus shares this urgency. "So if you are offering your gift at the altar and there remember that your brother has something against you, leave your gift there before the altar and go. First be reconciled to your brother, and then come and offer your gift" (Matt 5:23-24). Shockingly, Jesus tells Jews who have brought their sacrificial lamb to the priests to tie it up and leave it there. *Dealing with a problem is more urgent than worshiping God!* There could not be a higher priority.

If we are convinced that it is our brother's obligation to come to us—and we often cling to such justifications when we have been hurt—Jesus speaks to the opposite situation. "If your brother sins against you, go and tell him his fault, between you and him alone. If he listens to you, you have gained your brother" (Matt 18:15). Here is conflict resolution from the wounded side. The echoes of Leviticus 19:17-18 are here too, insisting that we need to "reason frankly" with our neighbor in hopes of dealing with the problem.

If you're keeping track at home, that means that whether we are the offending party (Matt 5:23-24) or the offended party (Matt 18:15), *it is still our obligation to go resolve the conflict. We deal with our problems*—whether we caused them or someone else did.

We hesitate with this. It seems like a lot of trouble. We're hurt and frustrated. We're convinced they would never listen to us. Or maybe that they deserve for us to shun them or treat them poorly. But in our hurt, we don't see that we are refusing to deal with something that Jesus teaches us to deal with urgently.

We all know of situations where a small slight or misunderstanding turns into a huge, long-lasting problem. A sharp word becomes a grudge. Bitterness is born and grows into malice and hatred. Feuds form that persist for years or sometimes generations. *What if someone just had the guts to say something?*

And we learn about the need for healthy relationships *at home*. We know that we make each other angry at times. We learn how to express that anger without sinning. We learn that relationships are not always easy and clean. They take work. We have to apologize and accept apologies. We deal with the consequences of our words. We correct and encourage and lead and follow.

Parents are teaching their children how to deal with—or not deal with—the problems they have with others. Do they see us argue and stay angry? Do we dig in and give full vent to our anger?

Do we go to them to resolve problems when they are upset? Or are we instilling in them our own strategies of conflict avoidance?

I am especially drawing attention to how our kids observe, digest, and mimic our own conflict strategies with our mates. Some marriages are loud and explosive, showing children that conflict is risky and intense. Other marriages show a different style, where hostility is latent and builds over time until it boils over. Some husbands and wives freeze each other out. This shows our kids how to explode at whatever triggers them—or how to grow coldly distant instead of dealing with problems. While we will never be perfect in how we handle conflict—and each style has its own strengths and weaknesses—I want to stress that *a strategy that fails to deal with real problems in the home is damaging to our relationships and teaches our children unhealthy habits.*

In Christian homes, we deal with our problems.

To Stop Sin Before It Spreads

When God instructs the Israelites to resolve their conflicts with each other, he adds an important motivation: "You shall reason frankly with your neighbor, lest you incur sin because of him" (Lev 19:17). We can "incur sin" when we choose the path of hatred over the path of "(reasoning) frankly." This does not mean that we bear the other person's sin or share in their guilt because of what they have done. The phrase can mean that we sin in response to their actions by growing to hate them ("you shall not hate your brother in your heart") or that we sin by failing to call him out. Either way, the focus of this phrase is on *how their sin can affect me.* What begins with something inappropriate *they* do can become a problem for *me.* If I don't want to incur sin, I need to deal with my problems. In doing so, I stop sin before it spreads—to me and others.

Just as there is an urgency to broken relationships—just as our frustrations with one another can worsen and spread—so there is a danger that when we don't deal with our problems, sin worsens and spreads.

This must be the reason behind the rule Jesus gives for his followers: "If your brother sins, rebuke him, and if he repents, forgive him, and if he sins against you seven times in the day, and turns to you seven times, saying, 'I repent,' you must forgive him" (Luke 17:3-4). Because we care about each other, we say something when we see sin in each other's lives. "If your brother sins, rebuke him" is Jesus' way of insisting that we deal with our problems out of concern for each other.

We rebuke when we see sin in each other's lives because *sin is different from someone annoying or upsetting me.* We easily get confused when we use the word "offend" in this context, since offense in the Bible (causing someone to stumble) is different from offense in our time (making someone feel upset). When people (yes, even family) annoy or upset me, they have not necessarily violated God's will. But sin is disobedience to God, which, left unaddressed, will jeopardize our relationship with him. Our motive in resolving our differences is not making others conform to our will, but to guard against sin. When someone sins, we address it so that it does not continue to grow, threaten their standing before God, and corrupt others.

Surprisingly, I have seen Christians use Jesus' words here in Luke 17 as a pretext *not* to forgive. Jesus is not teaching us about situations in which we don't forgive. He is instructing us about all the different situations in which we *should* forgive because we are faithfully dealing with our problems. He views Christian relationships as in constant need of maintenance, forgiveness, challenge, and reconciliation. *We don't want our brother to be lost, so we deal with our problems.*

A host of New Testament passages confirms this willingness to address sin we observe:

Take care, brothers, lest there be in any of you an evil, unbelieving heart, leading you to fall away from the living God. But exhort one another every day, as long as it is called 'today,' that none of you may be hardened by the deceitfulness of sin (Heb 3:12-13).

See to it that no one fails to obtain the grace of God; that no 'root of bitterness' springs up and causes trouble, and by it many become defiled; that no one is sexually immoral or unholy like Esau, who sold his birthright for a single meal (Heb 12:15-16).

Your boasting is not good. Do you not know that a little leaven leavens the whole lump? (1 Cor 5:6).

My brothers, if anyone among you wanders from the truth and someone brings him back, let him know that whoever brings back a sinner from his wandering will save his soul from death and will cover a multitude of sins (James 5:19-20).

There is urgency in the tone of the NT writers here. Watch out! Take care! Exhort ever day! Turn him back! Leaven will spread! Roots of bitterness will spring up! We deal with our problems because we cannot turn a blind eye to sin.

This does not mean that we are always hammering people who are struggling to do the right thing. These verses are not advocating beating up the weak, acting as if we're perfect, constantly bringing up old failures, or showing an unwillingness to let anything go. They are teaching us that *we recognize that sin is dangerous and we will do what we can to deal with it.*

How do we apply these truths at home? Christian homes need a vocabulary of sin. Some things need to be addressed because they disrupt the family, but others are addressed because they violate the will of a holy God. Some problems are fixed by an apology or a slight change of action; sin problems are fixed by change *and* some kind of acknowledgment and confession to God. Parents can model this: opening up to children when the parent has made a wrong choice that involves them, apologizing to them, and perhaps even praying for forgiveness in their presence. When the father has led the family in an inappropriate way, it might be wise to lead the family in confessional prayer.

In my judgment, it is important for Christian families to be very careful with our use of words like *sin, wrong, and evil*. These are loaded theological terms; they should not be thrown around to describe someone doing a crummy job cleaning the bathroom. "I did wrong" is a powerful confession; we should save it for times when it is true of moral wrong, so that it retains that power.

Further, when we comment on the choices of other families, great care should be taken with these terms. My family does not eat at Applebee's; other families are not "wrong" to do so. This silly illustration quickly turns more serious when the topic is not restaurants, but curfews, friends, dress, words, habits, and even beliefs of other families. There will always be differences between families, but not everything is a right/wrong divide.

The goal in all of this is to retain the sanctity of these biblical warnings. When I make the statement—of my kids, my wife, or myself—that someone has sinned, I want my family to understand the extreme seriousness of my words.

Stopping sin before it spreads, then, means that *Christian parents will be alert to trends of behavior in the home that are leading in the direction of sin*. Disrespect, dishonesty, unkindness, and rebellion will take various forms, some more pressing and intense than others. Discernment and wisdom will be required to know which issues are most important and when lines are crossed. But all of this is window dressing on the real question: Will we deal with our problems?

Most sins have shades of gray around them. Fornication is clearly sinful, but there are a lot of behaviors that are close to fornication without meeting the textbook definition. What exactly is profane speech? At what point is someone drunk? How do I know exactly when I'm proud or greedy? As Christian parents, we have the great privilege of building our homes to have a certain attitude toward sin. Are we teaching one another to get as close to the line as possible by ignoring the tendency until a major violation? Are we showing each other that sin is not really that big a deal—in our lives or in others'? Will we deal with our problems?

HOW DO WE DEAL WITH OUR PROBLEMS?

With Discernment

The Bible teaches us to be aware of the differences in people and situations and to seek to respond appropriately. Not every problem is a crisis.

"*Good sense makes one slow to anger, and it is his glory to overlook an offense*" (Prov 19:11). Some offenses can be overlooked without harm. They are not worth making a fuss over; they are just not that big a deal. They are not sin issues. Yet *we do not overlook these issues because we are scared to say something*. We acknowledge that the situation does not demand a strong response. We exercise discernment. There is virtue in not making every little annoyance or misstep into a problem. It is wise to be "slow to anger" and to "overlook an offense." This is just a survival skill in all homes.

The corollary is that *there are some things I need to learn to just let go*.

Discernment is also important as we determine the spiritual and emotional state of the person involved. "And we urge you, brothers, admonish the idle, encourage the fainthearted, help the weak, be patient with them all" (1 Thess 5:14). Paul wants the Thessalonians to distinguish between different groups of people (idle, fainthearted, weak). This requires deep thought and insight. The same inappropriate behavior might stem from one person being idle or unruly, while in another person it comes from weakness and discouragement. We will approach them differently. The rebellious person, we "admonish"; the tired, we "encourage"; the overburdened, we "help." There is no one-size-fits-all approach to people. Learning the right way to deal with others requires discernment.

Part of this is natural in a home. Instinctively, we treat an infant differently from a teenager. We know that the level of responsibility differs as children mature. But we need this discernment in determining the best approaches to discipline and confrontation.

When I first became a father, I felt the immense pressure of parental responsibility. I considered every decision to be of extreme importance to my son's future. If I let him get up from the table without finishing his meal, will he develop unhealthy eating habits? If he doesn't learn to share, will he have normal social skills? And most of all, if he doesn't do what I say in this instant, will he grow up to disobey God? Looking back on it now, I see that what I lacked was *discernment*—the wisdom to know which concerns were legitimate, what is age-appropriate, and the patience to continue to work with him through his maturation. So while on the one hand, the Bible teaches us to deal with problems, it also reminds us of the need to pick our battles, deciding carefully which problems we make into huge issues.

This is also true in the marriage relationship. When we first marry, we begin to notice the foibles of our mates. Little things annoy us. And of course the things that annoy our mates about us don't seem like that big a deal to us. My habit of watching football for an entire day each week doesn't seem problematic to me; my wife might disagree. I remember distinctly a surprisingly heated argument with my wife that centered around where I would place my briefcase when I got home from work. Just how much does that matter? We needed help with discernment. Since that time, we have developed a kind of code word that helps us understand whether something is truly worth a serious discussion. As we discuss plans or concerns, one of us will say, "this is very important to me." When we hear these words, we both know to listen more carefully and work to accommodate one another because this is not an ordinary request. *Learning how to pick our battles—and when to lay down our arms—is essential to an excellent marriage.*

Christian homes also need a climate of discernment. We don't scream every time someone does something we don't like. We teach about—and demonstrate—proportionate responses. We use words, not fists. What do we do when we're not getting along with someone? Parents, whatever discernment we show (or lack) is being absorbed by our children.

And as our kids grow, we can help them develop their own sense of discernment. We can involve them in the decision-making about their own issues. Would you like me to talk to your teacher? How do you think we should handle this? It is especially vital to help our kids work through the frustration phase ("no, Dad, that won't work either!") to move toward practical solutions for problems.

Meanwhile, there is always the underlying reality that *there are some things we need to learn to just let go.*

With Courage

Why don't we deal with our problems? Most of the time it's because we're scared. We have been hurt and we don't want to hurt again. We don't want to have a negative encounter. We don't know what the other person will say or do. Occasionally we are just so angry that we don't want to deal with them.

Every time we deal with a problem, we jeopardize the relationship. It is a crossroads. Will this relationship continue to be strong and healthy—or will this conflict end it?

Eli was the high priest of Israel whose two sons were also priests. But his sons were doing great evil and threatening the worship of God. Eli calls them in and rebukes them, but they continue to rebel.

God pronounces judgment on Eli: "And I declare to him that I am about to punish his house forever, for the iniquity that he knew, because his sons were blaspheming God, and he did not restrain them" (1 Sam 3:13). Eli could have done something stronger—removing his sons from their positions or publicly renouncing them. God is not pleased with Eli's tepid rebuke, asking him, "Why then do you…honor your sons above me…?" (1 Sam 2:29). *God expects Eli to care more about the compromised worship of God than his kids.* And so Eli fails because he lacks the courage to deal with his problems.

For all his virtues, King David has a similar failure with his children. When his son Adonijah attempts to seize the throne, the biblical author rebukes David's entire parental strategy: "His father had never at any time displeased him by asking, 'Why have you done thus and so?'" (1 Kings 1:6). Even after his indulgence with Absalom ends with a coup, David does not change his approach. He does not want to "displease" his son by challenging him about his behavior. David does not discipline his son, even when he needs to. Even though he has the remarkable courage to face down Goliath, David lacks the courage to deal with the problems in his own family.

These examples are daunting. The stakes are high. Where do we get the courage to deal with our problems? *We remember that some things are more important than whether people are happy with us.* The worship of God was more important than the damage Eli would do to his relationship with his sons. The stability of the kingdom was more important than David "displeasing" Adonijah by challenging him. For us, it is primarily the *long-term growth of our children* that is more important than their constant happiness. For us, it is the *long-term strength and stability of our marriage* that is more important than whether we need to have a hard conversation. The question of courage is: do we really care most about the long-term relationship? We deal with our problems with courage because we realize that *I just can't let this go without saying something. It's too important.*

Beyond that, it has helped me gain courage to know that *dealing with a problem is a far better approach than ignoring it*. We can make progress on the issue. I can quit stewing on it. I can move forward. If others reject my counsel, at least I can say that I've done what I could. So even though I am not a confrontational person, I have learned from experience to just get the cards on the table. Let's talk about it and work through it. Following Scripture in these areas has blessed me—and that gives me courage to say something.

With Humility

When we deal with a problem, we must resist the temptation to condescend and grow proud.

"Brothers, if anyone is caught in any transgression, you who are spiritual should restore him in a spirit of gentleness. Keep watch on yourself, lest you too be tempted" (Gal 6:1). When we must say something to someone about a problem, Paul insists on *"gentleness"* and warns us to keep an eye on our own hearts. We are not above anyone else—and the time will come when we are on the other side of this conversation.

"And the LORD's servant must not be quarrelsome but kind to everyone, able to teach, patiently enduring evil, correcting his opponents with gentleness" (2 Tim 2:24-25). We do not deal with problems because we love conflict ("quarrelsome"). Instead, we are patient, kind, and gentle. We refuse to just pick on people. The time will come when we are on the other side of this conversation.

And it may be that we are entirely wrong! It may be that our efforts to deal with the problem, our read on the situation, or our advice about what comes next are incorrect. "But the wisdom from above is first pure, then peaceable, gentle, open to reason, full of mercy and good fruits, impartial and sincere" (James 3:17). James insists that godly wisdom is "open to reason." Our minds are not made up. We are humble, eager to listen, and ready to have a brotherly dialogue with each other. We are willing to yield if we realize others are right and we are wrong.

It may be that, as we ask questions or express concerns, more information comes to light. Our initial impressions of the situation can be shown to be completely wrong. Or perhaps by further discussion we can be convinced of a completely different view. Soaking our discussions in humility will bless us and others.

A HOME THAT DEALS WITH OUR PROBLEMS

What does this look like in a home? Not every conflict has to be full of anger and yelling. But we *are* going to address the serious problems.

Christian homes will not be "sweep it under the rug" homes. We will not be "look the other way" homes. We will not be "living in denial" homes. We will face the truth, unpleasant though it may be.

Consider Mark and Maggie, a married couple.

MAGGIE: Mark, we need to talk about something.

MARK: Yikes. What's up?

MAGGIE: I feel like we never see each other. We're so busy that we never have any time together. It makes me—

MARK: Wait, what?! That's just not true! We see each other every day! Last week we had two nights where we didn't have anything going on!

MAGGIE: Yeah, because things got canceled! Don't act like you did that! It makes me feel distant from you. I don't know what you're thinking about and sometimes I don't know where you are and what you're doing. I work all day, then I come home, cook, take care of the kids, and clean. You show up whenever you feel like and then go hang out with your friends. It makes me angry.

MARK: You're just ungrateful! I'm here a lot but I just never do enough for you! We both have burdens. Just get over yourself!

(Maggie leaves the room in tears)

Mark shows a typical defensiveness. Instead of seeing his wife as having the courage to deal with a problem, he only hears criticism and shuts down. In a home that deals with its problems, that conversation might go a little more like this:

MAGGIE: Mark, we need to talk about something.

MARK: Yikes. What's up?

MAGGIE: I feel like we never see each other. We're so busy that we never have any time together. It makes me feel distant from you. I don't know what you're thinking about and sometimes I don't know where you are and what you're doing. I work all day, then I come home, cook, take care of the kids, and clean. You show up whenever you feel like and then go hang out with your friends. It makes me angry.

MARK: Whoa! That's a lot. I'm sorry you're feeling frustrated. I was feeling pretty good about things since we got to spend two days together last week.

MAGGIE: Yes, that was nice, but actual time together feels like a special occasion!

MARK: Are you saying you don't want to work or cook or clean? I don't understand.

MAGGIE: No, I'm saying it just all feels like too much and I don't feel like you help me with any of that.

MARK: OK, so if we were to change something, where could we cut back?

Notice how dealing with problems *takes determined effort from both parties*. It involves courage and humility from both to avoid defensiveness, suspend anger, and work through the tangle of issues involved. Sometimes it is easier to blow up or shut down than deal with an issue. In Christian homes, we seek to understand each other, open ourselves up to the possibility that we are wrong, and build toward mutually satisfying conclusions.

If there is a problem in our marriage, we will address it and work on it. We will work to stay connected with our spouses and make them happy. If we sense that someone is unhappy, we will move toward them rather than away. If we disapprove of our mate's behavior, we will tell them (while certainly differentiating between annoyances and serious issues). If we need to change, we will admit it and attempt to do so. We will not be embarrassed to seek help, admit that things are not ideal, or change drastically to bless our mate.

If there is a problem with our children, we will correct it and work through it. We will be humble and reasonable, but we will face our challenges. We will talk frankly with them about the issue. If we are concerned about our children's friends, we will address it. If we see a growing problem, we will work to stop it. We will build viable alternatives for them, provide attainable goals, and consistently work with them to resolve the issues.

If there is a problem outside the home, we will discuss how to deal with it. We will talk through what is appropriate for the situation—whether it involves parents or children. And we will encourage courageous action so that conflict does not continue.

Some homes are homes where we don't deal with our problems. Children grow up resenting parents. Destructive behaviors go unchecked. Frustration builds. Issues boil over from time to time, but they are never brought out into the open and dealt with head-on. Marriages grow cold. Inattention and disappointment lead to a "ships passing in the night" feeling. Meanwhile there are people outside our homes who are not like us. Sometimes they wrong someone in the family, so we all grow to hate them. We don't want to see them, but we love to talk about them negatively. A sinister spirit of "us against them" grows, but we are only unified by our hurt and condescension.

Some churches are churches where we don't deal with our problems. Grudges lay dormant for many years, slowly draining the energy from a group. Hard words are never resolved and continue to cut us, but we never say anything to the actual person who hurt us. As the years pass, it seems petty to even bring it up, but it still bothers us. New people join the group, but they sense the undercurrent of bitterness, anger, and malice. And it's only a matter of time before we get cross with *them* and the pattern repeats.

God calls us to be a people who deal with their problems.

I don't like confrontation—and I suspect you don't either. Yet it can be healthy, a blessing to us and others, and is part of the will of God.

We deal with our problems.

For Personal Introspection

- Am I a conflict avoider? In what situations am I reluctant to bring up issues that need to be dealt with?
- Do I have grudges against anyone? Have I attempted to resolve these differences?
- What was the strategy for confrontation in the home of my youth? How has that influenced me today?
- How can I gain the courage to correct and confront?

For Discussion

- Do healthy relationships involve conflict? What is the difference between a healthy and unhealthy approach to conflict?
- What are some of the main reasons why people struggle to deal with their problems with others?
- How do we know when an issue should be discussed and when it should be ignored?
- What are some ways we can show humility when addressing issues with others?

RULE 8

We Lead by Serving

Jesus calls his people to be different. He tells his disciples that they are the light of the world and a city set on a hill and the salt of the earth (Matt 5:13-16). Paul tells Christians, "Do not be conformed to this world, but be transformed by the renewal of your mind" (Rom 12:2). But this differentness is not elitism; we are not different because we are inherently superior. *Jesus calls his people to be different because they listen to God rather than the voices of their fellowmen.*

When Jesus corrects his disciples, it is with this understood assumption. At one point, James and John lobby Jesus for the right and left hand (positions of great influence) in his coming kingdom. Jesus refuses to promise them such positions. Instead, he calls the entire group together and teaches.

> And Jesus called them to him and said to them, 'You know that those who are considered rulers of the Gentiles LORD it over them, and their great ones exercise authority over them. But it shall not be so among you. But whoever would be great among you must be your servant, and whoever would be first among you must be slave of all. For even the Son of Man came not to be served but to serve, and to give his life as a ransom for many' (Mark 10:42-45).

James and John's power play has demonstrated something corrupt within them. This desire to have power and influence over others, to gain control, to seek status, and to be great is not God's will for them. Instead, this is the behavior of the "rulers of the Gentiles"—people who do not even know the true God. They seek out positions, schmooze and politick for them, and abuse power when they attain it. They want to be great.

Jesus then utters words which are the clarion call to something higher—words that belong etched into the lintels of every Christian home: "it shall not be so among you." Jesus calls us to something higher than leadership by gaining power, controlling others, and making demands. He calls us to lead by serving.

He could be speaking to our time. Our culture focuses on leadership by fighting to get to the top of the heap in business, in entertainment, and in politics. Who has the most followers? Who has the greatest influence? Who has the most money? Who has true power? These are our cultural leaders—the people whom we believe deserve to be respected, listened to, and obeyed. Jesus calls us to be different—to seek a different path to change lives, engage with others, and lead them appropriately. "But whoever would be great among you must be your servant, and whoever would be first among you must be slave of all" (Mark 10:43-44). We lead by serving.

Christian homes are positioned to influence the world, feeding into it a set of Christlike people with radically countercultural ideas. Truly making a difference will not come from clawing our way to the top, then forcing everyone to listen to Jesus. It will come when we lead by serving.

But that also means that we must make service a priority in our homes, passing on this new way of thinking to a new generation. *We lead by serving.*

AT HOME WE LEARN THE VIRTUE OF SERVICE

As Jesus corrects these power-hungry disciples, he urges them to channel all of their energy and desperate need for validation into a desire to serve.

"But whoever would be great among you must be your servant, and whoever would be first among you must be slave of all. For even the Son of Man came not to be served but to serve, and to give his life as a ransom for many" (Mark 10:43-45). True greatness is found in service. The one who longs to be first must instead make himself the slave of everyone. At the forefront (or at the rear of the line, if you prefer) is Jesus, who came to earth and devoted his entire life to a powerful mission of service.

The problem is that we really don't believe this. It rolls off our tongues a little too easily. We don't really believe that the greatest people are the servants. As a culture, we give lipservice to the Mother Teresas of our world, admiring their devotion to taking care of others and their lives of renunciation. But we actually *emulate* the people who seek power, money, and influence at any cost. And these people—the power-grabbers—are the ones we listen to, follow, and admire. *They* are the ones whose books we buy, whose podcasts we download, and whose wealth we envy. Honest soul-searching is in order here. *If we are going to stem the tide of incredible selfishness, self-promotion, and self-fixation, we must establish the virtue of service.*

Service is a good thing. It is worth our time and energy. It is not something we do to get ahead. We do it merely to help others and honor Jesus.

We Give Instead of Getting

Paul reminds the Ephesians of a famous saying of Jesus: "In all things I have shown you that by working hard in this way we must help the weak and remember the words of the LORD Jesus, how he himself said, 'It is more blessed to give than to receive'" (Acts 20:35). Service has this inverted posture: we give instead of getting. We appear to have less, but we actually have more. When we give away our time and effort, we end up with something of much greater value: the blessing of helping others, the strengthening of relationships, and the joy of bringing glory to God rather than hoarding our gifts. It is more blessed to give than to receive.

There is an instinctual barrier here. From early ages (and even before birth!), we shower our kids with gifts. Parents have the ability to give kids things they can't get for themselves. Over and over, year after year, the pattern of getting, getting, getting is reinforced in the child's mind. Rarely, if ever, is a child called on to *give*—and if they are, it is often met with a baffled resistance. What's in it for me? Why would I do that? Without even realizing it, we train our children that getting is better than giving. *We must actively teach and lead our children to a different thought process.*

There is also a cultural barrier here. We have societal expectations of what we are entitled to. We look around at other families and assume that whatever *they* have is what *we* should have. We deserve it. I have watched this list of entitlements grow in my short life—it now involves phones, on-demand television, free time, cars, and spending cash. I am sure it will continue to grow. Most young people expect these things without giving anything to get them. But, of course, it is not only kids. American adults also want in on the gravy train, feeling that they are entitled to own the houses, cars, gadgets, and clothes they want. If ever we cannot have all that we want, we moan and complain as if suffering real hardship. *With all this focus on what we are getting, who has time for service? What's in it for me?*

At home we learn that *there is value in giving to others without any hope of return.*

We return again to Jesus.

And if you do good to those who do good to you, what benefit is that to you? For even sinners do the same. And if you lend to those from whom you expect to receive, what credit is that to you? Even sinners lend to sinners, to get back the same amount. But love your enemies, and do good, and lend, expecting nothing in return, and your reward will be great, and you will be sons of the Most High, for he is kind to the ungrateful and evil (Luke 6:33-35).

Notice that Jesus contrasts his values with the world, specifically the behavior of *"sinners."* It is understandable that *"sinners"* are always on the lookout for themselves, but Jesus calls his people to be different. We do good without worrying about whether we will receive good in return. We lend without expecting to be repaid. *These are the values of the kingdom of Jesus and they are the values that must undergird Christian homes.*

We Look for Opportunities to Do Good

Notice that Jesus teaches his disciples not only to love, but to "do good" (Luke 6:35). This is one of those phrases that seems too simple to deserve much attention. But it is the way New Testament authors often describe an outward-focused life of service. We follow a Savior who "went about doing good" (Acts 10:38) and we seek opportunities to imitate him.

> See that no one repays anyone evil for evil, but *always seek to do good* to one another and to everyone (1 Thess 5:15, emphasis mine).

> So then, as we have opportunity, *let us do good to everyone*, and especially those who are of the household of faith (Gal 6:10, emphasis mine).

To the contrary, 'if your enemy is hungry, feed him; if he is thirsty, give him something to drink; for by so doing you will heap burning coals on his head.' Do not be overcome by evil, but *overcome evil with good* (Rom 12:20-21, emphasis mine).

Do not neglect to *do good* and to share what you have, for such sacrifices are pleasing to God (Heb 13:16, emphasis mine).

We live in a world full of upset, hurt, angry people. From time to time they lash out and hurt us. We are an anxious, polarized, and dispirited nation. The focus of these passages is that *we cannot allow the tone of our world to overwhelm us*. Do not be overcome by evil, but overcome evil with good.

So the pressing question for Christians in our time—particularly within our homes—is *what are we doing today that is good?* Paul stresses that doing good will largely be based on the unique circumstances we encounter. We can only do good "as we have opportunity" (Gal 6:10). Yet Christian homes must practice awareness of the regular opportunities for doing good that present themselves to us. How can we do good?

We cannot start too early in teaching and practicing service in our homes. One way we can do that is by opening up our homes to others and allow them into our private spaces. It is one thing for you to see me when I have dressed myself well; it is quite another for you to hang out in the place where my dog eats and the carpet is stained and my kids have rubbed toothpaste on the wall. But we offer hospitality because *people need companionship in deep ways and we want to do them good.*

We can offer others our time and energy and effort. Whom can we visit? Who needs their yard mowed? Who is having a hard time? How can I do something kind—helpful—good for them? We serve others, but not because we have to. We serve others, but not because they pay us. We serve others *because we want to do good, like Jesus.*

Doing good can also involve each other. We can take turns helping one another with chores and responsibilities around the home to give each other a break. We can express gratitude when others make sacrifices for us. We can do simple kindnesses to serve each other, like getting someone's food, telling each other what their best traits are, or simply encouraging each other when we are feeling down.

Sometimes our good involves money. I find this challenging. Jesus tells us to give without sounding a trumpet or letting others know what we are doing (Matt 6:2-4), yet sometimes my family needs to know that *we* (as a family) are doing something good for others. All families must make decisions about whether, when, and how much to give. We may not be able to help every single needy person financially, but *there should at least be some times when our love and talk becomes real action.* Our kids, wives, and neighbors need to see that we are willing to sacrifice to do good.

Parents lead the way for their kids in this. Children learn by observation that service is a way of life in their family. They see Mom and Dad serving each other, serving them, serving in the church, serving in the neighborhood, and serving in the world. In families with multiple children (like ours), a transition must take place. Instead of focusing on fairness (he got one and I didn't!), kids must be taught to think in terms of service (you can have mine!). As time passes, a family culture develops. We learn the pleasure that comes from doing good things because they are good. We take the focus off of ourselves and put it onto others. Like Jesus, we go about doing good.

AT HOME WE LEARN THE NATURE OF REAL LEADERSHIP

When Jesus corrects James and John for their power-hungry ways, he does more than talk about service. He is also teaching us what it means to really lead others. "For even the Son of Man came not to be served but to serve, and to give his life as a ransom for many" (Mark 10:45). Jesus is our LORD and Master, yet he *leads by serving*.

Even as we read this, I suspect we have some lingering doubts. *Can people actually lead that way?* Serving other people sounds good, but you can't lead by serving in a business, right? Or as an elder? Or in government? And so the best test of Jesus' words and their feasibility happens *at home*.

Real Leadership Serves

The night of Jesus' betrayal—when the cross is looming the next day, when his disciples are gathered around eating the Last Supper, when Judas is preparing to sell him out—Jesus has an essential lesson to teach. He gets up from the table, takes off his outer cloak, puts on a towel, pours out some water, and begins to wash the feet of his disciples. He rolls up his sleeves. He does not tell one of the other disciples to do it. He doesn't call a servant. He does it himself. He gets his own hands dirty.

The scene is even more shocking when we remember who Jesus is. Can we imagine a president getting down on his knees and serving like this? (Imagine his poll numbers!). Can we imagine a king? A business guru? This is what Jesus calls attention to:

> You call me Teacher and LORD, and you are right, for so I am. If I then, your LORD and Teacher, have washed your feet, you also ought to wash one another's feet. For I have given you an example, that you also should do just as I have done to you. Truly, truly, I say to you, a servant is not greater than his master, nor is a messenger greater than the one who sent him (John 13:13-16).

The lesson is impressive because of Jesus' status. The Lord and Teacher serves like this, so we are never above service. We are not greater than he is. This is true leadership.

Real leadership is not bossing people around to do things we don't want to do. Real leadership rolls up its own sleeves. Real leadership doesn't ask others to help because we are unwilling to do it ourselves. There will be times when people need to see us serving if we're going to lead them. That includes our homes.

We are never too good to serve others in whatever sweaty, dirty, tedious form that takes. Positions of authority are not an excuse for laziness or pettiness. When we serve alongside others, we show that leadership is about passion for the goal, not a desire to boss others around.

Real Leadership Loves

John stresses that Jesus' foot-washing act stems from love (John 13:1). He loves these men and wants them to grow and humble themselves. He leads and serves from a heart of love.

Paul writes the Philippians, concerned that they are growing overly focused on themselves:

> So if there is any encouragement in Christ, any comfort from love, any participation of the Spirit, any affection and sympathy, complete my joy by being of the same mind, having the same love, being in full accord and of one mind. Do nothing from selfish ambition or conceit, but in humility count others more significant than yourselves. Let each of you look not only to his own interests, but also to the interests of others. Have this mind among yourselves, which is yours in Christ Jesus (Phil 2:1-5).

He wants them to "(have) the same love" and to abandon "selfish ambition" and to "in humility count others more significant than yourselves." Love is emphatically not focused on itself.

This way of thinking is characteristic of Jesus (Phil 2:5). Jesus demonstrates complete abandonment of his own will—leaving behind the privileges of his status (Phil 2:6-8) to suffer as a human. Why? *Jesus is driven by our deep need.* He has compassion on the crowds. They are like sheep without a shepherd. The harvest is white, but the laborers are few. They do not need to go away. He leaves the privileges of heaven to come and serve us. He chooses the obscurity of Nazareth. He associates with ne'er-do-wells and fishermen and lepers. He does it all to help and bless and redeem others. *Jesus spends and is spent for people.*

This is true leadership: *lowering ourselves in love.*

Leadership is best when it is directed, affected, and motivated by love. God does not give us relationships (or leadership opportunities) just so that we can have underlings and power. He gives us leadership so that we can *watch out for others and help them.* When we lead with love, *other people's needs become our focus.* We count others more significant than ourselves. Am I meeting their needs? Am I helping them? Providing for them? What more can I do for them? How can I help? How can I do them good?

This is the pattern of Christian relationships. Husbands lead their wives, but their primary command is to "love your wives, as Christ loved the church and gave himself up for her" (Eph 5:25). His role as "head of the wife" (Eph 5:23) is tempered by the fact that he cares deeply for and acts in the best interests of his wife. Leading in a marriage is not an excuse for domineering. Like Jesus, leaders lower themselves in love to serve others.

Parents lead their children, but not in a cruel or overbearing way. We raise them in "the discipline and instruction of the LORD" (Eph 6:4) because we love them.

Elders lead local churches, "not domineering over those in your charge, but being examples to the flock" (1 Pet 5:3). God does not intend this leadership role to be a reign of terror. Elders don't force the people to follow them; they lead in love. They lead by serving.

Often our leadership—I am thinking especially of times when we are just getting the feel of how to lead—is marked by our own weaknesses and insecurities. We feel that we have to throw our weight around. We lash out when others don't want to follow us. We try to force things. We demand respect. In our confusion and fear, we begin to act a lot more like the Gentiles who "lord it over" each other than followers of Jesus. Leading by lowering ourselves in love will be an exercise in faith.

Practically, this means that Christian husbands and wives serve one another. We faithfully communicate and accommodate one another as we divide up family duties. We pick up each other's slack. We make decisions to best suit each other. This is not only about holding down the fort so that our mate can enjoy their hobby of choice, but also sacrificing our time and money to help each other achieve what matters most to them. Instead of insisting on "my needs," I look out for my mate. When I do this, something amazing happens. Confident that I act out of sincere love for her, she begins to respond in love to me. A cycle of love and kindness begins. To be sure, things don't always run smoothly—and all of us battle selfishness—but marriage is a place where we demonstrate that *no one is above serving*.

Our children (ideally) see this. They also see when their parents are willing to serve them. We can show them—the more clearly stated, the better—that we factor their needs and desires into our decision-making. Parents can show their children that no one is above God's law; when we do wrong, we are just as wrong as kids are. This is not about some role reversal or youth-worship, but simply a way that we model humility to them. We do not require of our children what we are unwilling to do ourselves—whether that is taking out the trash or telling the truth.

We lead our kids by lowering ourselves in love. All our discipline is couched in our deep love for them. As much as possible, we must show them that our instructions are not based on a hunger for power and control over them. (After all, the time will come when that control ends and only their character will remain). Our goal is to lead *them* to do what *they* should by *us* doing what *we* should.

It also helps when we show our children the value in others who are leading by serving. It is easy to be critical of leaders. We complain loudly about the government, bosses, elders, and even parents in other families. *Can we breed positivity by showing good examples of selfless leaders? Can we point our families toward the good we see instead of complaining about the bad?*

In our homes, we have the tremendous privilege of learning and practicing selflessness. We have the honor of showing the brilliance and effectiveness of Jesus' model of servant leadership to ourselves, one another, and the world. We have incredible opportunities to do good, show kindness, and do God's will as it is done in heaven.

Can we imagine a world with servant leadership? A world where parents and children work together to do good within and outside the home? A world where elders are supported as they watch over the church? A world where businesses are run by bosses who care deeply about their employees and are always trying to improve their lives? A world where politicians are focused on how their constituents are doing—not to get re-elected, but because they love us?

Can we see what a blessing it would be to eliminate that spirit of competition and ambition that poisons our interactions and leadership structures? Can we see where Jesus wants to take us?

Jesus calls us to be different. Let's start that process in our homes.

We lead by serving.

For Personal Introspection

- Do I consider myself an ambitious person? In what ways do I want to be the "greatest"?
- What are some ways I can "do good" in my daily routine?
- What roles of leadership do I have? Do I ever act out of insecurity and fear? What am I afraid of?
- Am I serving the people in my home?

For Discussion

- How is service an antidote for selfishness? How have you seen this work?
- In what ways is giving better than getting?
- What should we learn from Jesus' example of washing the disciples' feet? How have you seen leadership like this?
- How does this model of leading by serving affect our parenting?

RULE

9

We Control Ourselves

The Proverbs have a way of phrasing things in ways that are hard to argue.

> "If you have found honey, eat only enough for you, lest you have your fill of it and vomit it" (Prov 25:16).

> "Let your foot be seldom in your neighbor's house, lest he have his fill of you and hate you" (Prov 25:17).

> "It is not good to eat much honey, nor is it glorious to seek one's own glory. A man without self-control is like a city broken into and left without walls" (Prov 25:27-28).

Honey is delicious, but too much makes us sick. Visiting our friend is nice, but if we are there too often, it becomes a problem. While this may sound like random advice, there is a principle undergirding it all: "A man without self-control is like a city broken into and left without walls." What is lacking when we are constantly overindulging and overstaying our welcome is self-control.

To the ancient mind, a city without walls is ripe for the picking. It lacks any defenses. It is susceptible to any passing army or group of bandits. No major offensive or long-term siege will be required; it is ready to fall. When we lack self-control, we are setting ourselves up for disaster. The exact problem may change—it may be our mouths or our use of money or our lust or our anger—but it is only a matter of time before we are overcome.

Home is the place where we practice building defenses against the evils that we encounter. Christian parents often attempt to protect their children by sheltering them from the temptations of the world. I am not critical of this approach (generally), but I find it to be both overwhelming and insufficient. How can I possibly identify all the potential issues my kids will face? How can they be ready for every situation? What if a temptation slips through the cracks?

Instead of mere prevention, Christian homes should aim at teaching and practicing self-control. *We control ourselves.*

THE ORIGIN OF SELF-CONTROL: LIBERATION

One of the most common images in the New Testament for those who are in sin is *slavery*. Jesus states that "everyone who practices sin is a slave to sin" (John 8:34). Paul contends that before coming to Christ, we were "slaves to various passions and pleasures" (Titus 3:3). Slavery means that even when we want to do better and be different, we continue to find ourselves stuck in the same problems. Like a slave unable to work his way to freedom, we begin to despair. Like a slave unable to work his way to freedom, we need a redeemer.

So when we were slaves to sin, what changed? Did we work our way out of that? Did we suddenly decide to be more disciplined and get our act together? Did we start waking up earlier, dieting, and cleaning up our language? No, what changed was that *he saved us.* He set us free.

When Paul describes his old actions under the Law of Moses, he says that he was "of the flesh, sold under sin" (Rom 7:14). He couldn't even do the things he *wanted* to do: "For I do not do what I want, but I do the very thing I hate" (Rom 7:15). What changed? How did he get out of his slavery? "Who will deliver me from this body of death? Thanks be to God through Jesus Christ our LORD" (Rom 7:24-25). By the grace of Jesus, Paul was set free (Rom 8:2).

Paul portrays the Gentiles' descent into sin as a powerful downward spiral. They move from ingratitude to selfishness to idolatry to sexual excess to the "debased mind" (Rom 1:18-32). What stops their cycle? Not their effort! It is only Jesus revealing the goodwill of God on sinful man (Rom 3:21-26).

Some of the Corinthians were sexually immoral, idolaters, thieves, greedy, and drunkards. What changed? "And such were some of you. But you were washed, you were sanctified, you were justified in the name of the LORD Jesus Christ and by the Spirit of our God" (1 Cor 6:11). They were set free.

He tells the Ephesians that they were "dead in the trespasses and sins in which you once walked" (Eph 2:1) and "carrying out the desires of the body and the mind, and were by nature children of wrath, like the rest of mankind" (Eph 2:3). What changed? Did they just get tired of that life? "But God…made us alive together with Christ" (Eph 2:4, 5). God acted to save them and set them free.

Why do I keep saying the same thing over and over? I want to stress that *self-control is not natural.* What is natural is for us to get *out* of control and become enslaved to sin. When we are enslaved to sin, we find it impossible to make serious, permanent change to the major problems of our lives on our own. This does not mean that when we are in sin, we are incapable of doing good or that our wills are broken by depravity. It means that *when we submit ourselves as slaves to sin (Rom 6:13, 16), we forfeit our ability to make lasting change.* Sin makes us slaves. Period. But self-control begins with liberation.

So the message of the New Testament is that *Christians should no longer be slaves of sin.* "We know that our old self was crucified with him in order that the body of sin might be brought to nothing, so that we would no longer be enslaved to sin. For one who has died has been set free from sin" (Rom 6:6-7). Or again, "let not sin therefore reign in your mortal body, to make you obey its passions" (Rom 6:12). We have been set free. Jesus has given us the sacrifice, power, wisdom, and family to help us be free. We can do this, but it is never on our own.

So when we are ensnared by pornography and feel hopelessly addicted, *we need to be set free*. When we are addicted to alcohol and substances—when we struggle to control our speech—when we are consumed with hatred—*we need to be set free*. We may still feel those impulses and struggles. Yet we can know that we are forgiven, take them seriously, confess them to others, set up systems to hold us accountable, and make real change. Behind all this change is Jesus, our liberator.

How does this play out in our homes? It starts with *intense honesty* between husbands and wives *about our self-control issues*. Our inability to control ourselves directly affects our mate. If my spending is out of control, my wife will suffer. If I cannot control my eating, substance use, spending, or temper, my mate already knows and is deeply impacted. Especially we must fight the tendency we have to either hide or downplay self-control problems ("it's not that big a deal" or "it's not as bad as so-and-so" or "you're no angel either"). The goal is to work together so that Jesus is honored by our personal and family choices.

This proceeds into a *continual family conversation about the level of self-control in the family*. This is not restricted to parents or any one person. Our family has consistent resets about how we are doing in terms of control. How clean is our home? How much have we been spending? How are we eating (eating out too much, eating too much pizza/candy, etc)? Are we exercising? Are we spending too much time on screens? These are regular struggles for Mom and Dad as well as kids. Underlying the discussion is the sense that too much honey is not good. We don't like the feeling we get when we're out of control. We start to feel bad physically. When we exercise, we start to feel good. When eating out is a privilege we work toward, we enjoy it more. Sometimes (usually right after the holidays!) we struggle through a month or two of "family austerity." No one is exempt. With these conversations, we are reinforcing the concept of balance and move our children toward the goal of self-moderation.

Meanwhile, *parents reinforce the narrative that we have personally been out of control in the past (which led us into sin), but Jesus has set us free for better things.* The reason why we work so hard to control ourselves is not just because it feels better. There is a spiritual dimension that this satisfaction reflects. God wants us to be in control and has set us free for that purpose. I am not suggesting that parents must continuously detail the nature of their sinful past, but I do believe that we should represent ourselves to our kids as redeemed sinners. So while our children may not (at their youngest ages) yet understand what it is to be liberated from slavery to sin, they can grow up knowing that one of the dimensions of sin is rejecting God's limits and control. Their years of training in self-control will also show them how good and right it will feel to admit the problem and seek God's help so that they can regain control over themselves.

THE CHARACTER OF SELF-CONTROL: RULING MY SPIRIT

"Whoever is slow to anger is better than the mighty, and he who rules his spirit than he who takes a city" (Prov 16:32).

This proverb links being "slow to anger" with "he who rules his spirit." The one who is careful about letting himself grow angry is "better than the mighty." He is in control of himself, which is even more difficult than physically controlling others. Ruling our spirits makes us better "than he who takes a city." There is a lot of strategy and intelligence required in conquering a city, but self-control is harder.

I find this image particularly helpful because it takes all the accolades and admiration we give to military heroes and transfers it to our inner battles. *If I can rule my spirit, I will have won an even more impressive victory.*

Paul encourages Timothy to prepare for some coming opposition: "For this reason I remind you to fan into flame the gift of God, which is in you through the laying on of my hands, for God gave us a spirit not of fear but of power and love and self-control" (2 Tim 1:6-7). Paul seems to think that Timothy is in danger of growing weak and tentative, so he tells him not to be ashamed (2 Tim 1:8), but to be strengthened (2 Tim 2:1). The encouragement is that *God didn't give us a spirit of fear.* He does not intend us to be afraid of the world or of sin. *He gave us a spirit of power, love, and self-control.* That last word is sometimes translated as "a sound mind" or "discipline." Self-control is about us growing powerful. We are suddenly free to be in charge of our lives again, under the leadership of Christ. Where sin has reigned, we now can rule our spirits.

Paul also describes to the Corinthians his willingness to forgo his rights for the sake of those he is trying to teach. Why?

> Do you not know that in a race all the runners run, but only one receives the prize? So run that you may obtain it. Every athlete exercises self-control in all things. They do it to receive a perishable wreath, but we an imperishable. So I do not run aimlessly; I do not box as one beating the air. But I discipline my body and keep it under control, lest after preaching to others I myself should be disqualified (1 Cor 9:24-27).

He is willing to give up certain things because he thinks of himself as running a race. Those who run to win have to completely dedicate themselves to the race. They sacrifice a lot to be prepared for the competition ("every athlete exercises self-control in all things"). They take great care of their bodies. They train continually. They watch their diets. They say no to many things because they want to win. Paul wants to win like that—to win the *eternal* prize—and so he will suffer a little now.

Practically, Paul says that "I discipline my body and keep it under control." The Greek here is vivid; Paul says that he punches or pummels his body and makes it his slave. He is not advocating self-abuse. He is asserting control over his body. He will control himself—even forfeiting things that are not wrong in themselves—to make sure that his body is *his* slave, not the other way around. I don't serve my body; my body serves me. I am in control, not my body. I don't have to do what my body (or even my passing thought) desires. Under the lordship of Jesus, I am in control. My body must do what I tell it, pleasant or unpleasant. I have been given dominion over myself again. Paul shows how Christians should rule their spirits.

Beginning here, we apply self-control to each area of our lives. I will rule my spirit about anger. Just because I feel a certain way doesn't mean that I can act out of anger, hurt others, say evil words, or behave myself in an unchristian way. (We will have more to say about anger in the next chapter).

I will rule my spirit about sexual desires. Just because I have a desire or thought doesn't mean that I must act out of it.

I will rule my spirit about food and drink. Just because I want certain things—or want them at certain times—doesn't mean that I must have them.

I will rule my spirit about words. Just because I feel like saying something—or it would make me feel good—or it seems justified—doesn't meant that I must. *I* will make those choices.

I will rule my spirit about doing good. I will serve, give encouragement, pray, and work because I have voluntarily chosen to do good in honor of my God.

There is an irony here. Our world often ridicules people who are in control of themselves. They mock when we abstain from sinful and harmful situations and activities. They venerate the free-spending, free-wheeling, anything-goes personality and mock Christians as buttoned-down, puritanical, and repressed. Scripture flips that script. *There is no virtue or value in being a slave of every whim that crosses our mind. There is value in ruling my spirit.*

So while the world tells us that self-control means being enslaved and not having any fun, the Bible teaches that *self-control is the way to true freedom.* The world says that controlled people can't do what they want; the Bible says that uncontrolled people are primed for a fall. The world says that with self-control, you have to say no to yourself; the Bible says that with self-control, *you finally* can *say no to yourself.*

In addition, it is only in self-control that I can achieve the things I long to achieve. "Every athlete exercises self-control in all things. They do it to receive a perishable wreath, but we an imperishable" (1 Cor 9:25). By choosing a goal (winning gold in the marathon), we choose to limit other options (having tons of milkshakes). No matter how much I want gold, if I keep drinking those milkshakes, I won't get there. I need self-control to accomplish my goals. Yet when I can say no to me, I can pursue higher things. Only when I rule my spirit do I have true freedom.

SELF-CONTROL IN THE HOME

So how do we teach and model self-control in our homes? How do we encourage the ruling of our spirits?

We Practice Limits

All homes need limits and boundaries because *all people do* (yes, even adults!). Christian homes need limits on how much we can play our games, how long we are going to be awake, and how much junk food we are going to eat. In most cases, limits are not about these things being wrong or even bad. *Limits teach us how to tell ourselves no.* "If you have found honey, eat only enough for you, lest you have your fill of it and vomit it" (Prov 25:16). Even when we are eating honey, there must be a point where we declare that we have had enough and push the plate away.

Children are not born with limits. They must be taught and shown—and retaught and reshown—where the boundary lines are. Some of that process is about learning to respect parental authority, but some of it is about learning how to regulate themselves. *Our goal in creating and enforcing limits is to teach our kids how to push the plate away for themselves.* The time will come when my kids leave my home and my restrictions on what they eat and watch and do will end. What happens then? Am I building in them the capacity to rule their own spirits?

Parents of young children need patience with the consistent testing of the limits they set for their kids. As they age, we can extend bedtimes or allow more candy bars, stressing that respecting limits builds trust. Parents can also keep talking with their children about the goal: "The reason that I want you to only play on the tablet for 30 minutes is that I want you to be able to limit your usage when you have your own phone." "Even Mom and Dad have to tell themselves no to things they want to do." Limits help put self-control in concrete terms for kids.

I would also caution parents about having a very different set of rules for themselves than for their kids. Of course it is natural for the limits to be different for adults, but if parents watch whatever they want, eat whatever they want, and play as long as they want, then it may undermine the lesson we are attempting to teach. Our kids may simply learn that they have to have limits now, but when they are grown, they can do whatever they want. Christian homes have limits because *all people need them.*

We Practice Rhythms

God made the world to work in rhythms. "While the earth remains, seedtime and harvest, cold and heat, summer and winter, day and night, shall not cease" (Gen 8:22). Life on earth hinges on these alternating cycles. Human life also works in rhythms. "For everything there is a season, and a time for every matter under heaven: a time to be born, and a time to die; a time to plant, and a time to pluck up what is planted; a time to kill, and a time to heal…a time to weep, and a time to laugh" (Ecclesiastes 3:1-3, 4). Life demands certain responses from us as it cycles from life to death. Things are not always great, nor are they always terrible. Things are not always happy, nor are they always sad. Back and forth goes the rhythm.

And when we go against the grain of the rhythms God has placed in the world, it goes poorly for us. When God made the world, he set aside the seventh day as a day of rest (Gen 2:2, Ex 20:8-11). He placed this rhythm in us: we do not always work. Sometimes we rest. But we also do not always rest. Most of the time we work. If we work during our rest time, we ruin our health and our relationships. If we rest during our work time, we become lazy, unproductive, and poor. We must embrace the rhythms of life.

There are certain rhythms that help us with self-control—and many of them can be a part of home life. Here are a few of my suggestions from our home:

We work before we play. Play is good, but play is not the purpose of life. We want to meet our responsibilities (at whatever stage of life we are in) before we focus on entertainment. In our home, we have made chores, exercise, and homework prerequisites to play and free time. Our goal is to develop a sense of restraint and to tap into the natural rhythm of the world that we can only rest when our work is complete. When the kids leave home, we want them to be formed as adults who instinctively seek to work before play.

We thank God before we eat. Jesus prays before eating (Matt 14:19, 26:26) and Paul says that no food "is to be rejected if it is received with thanksgiving, for it is made holy by the word of God and prayer" (1 Tim 4:4-5). Each time we eat, we reinforce that what we have is to be "received with thanksgiving." Of course this can become a mindless ritual, but when properly done, it is a helpful acknowledgment of God's goodness and a way to keep God in our daily thinking. My kids will eat for the rest of their lives; I want them to have the rhythm of seeing God's goodness each time they do.

We ask permission before doing something questionable. As children mature, they learn the basic rules of what Mom and Dad want for them. Some actions are safe: they don't need to ask to go to the bathroom (once they are able!). But other actions are questionable, either because they are not sure what their parents think about it or because they suspect it is not good. In our home, we always want to reinforce that it is OK to ask us before you do it. Of course this creates its own difficulties—the sheer number of requests (especially with multiple children) can wear us down—but the goal is for kids to learn to ask for permission rather than just forging ahead.

The reason for these rhythms is that *we want these to be the rhythms they embrace for the rest of their lives.* Playing before working is dangerous for *adults*! And maybe adults don't always ask permission for what they do, but they are subject to God. That momentary hesitation—when we consider a potential activity and ask whether we *should* do something—is something I want ingrained in my kids.

We Practice Boundaries

There are space boundaries, where one member of the family should respect the personal space of another. There are ownership boundaries—some things are mine and some are yours—that must be observed. There are appropriateness boundaries, which stress that some actions or words are untoward or do not fit the situation.

Boundaries help us learn respect for each other, as we've discussed previously, but they also reinforce self-control. I don't get to go wherever I want, take all your things, or talk about inappropriate things. I must control myself to remain within my boundaries and respect yours.

One of the most difficult parts of teaching self-control is the fact that *I can undermine it all when I, as a parent, don't practice it.* When I don't limit myself—or I go against the rhythms God has placed in the world—or I violate the boundaries of others—it is frustrating to the whole family. Christian parents must answer a probing question: *Am I teaching them self-control, or am I merely teaching my kids that they have to be self-controlled until they get to be adults?* Do I show by my own lack of control that childhood is a probationary period—that once they are grown, they will finally be free to play on their phones all day, eat junk food all the time, blow all their money on their own interests, show no concern for anyone else, and be masters of their own destiny? My spouse and kids see the real me. They know how I live. And I cannot teach them what I am unwilling to practice.

Yet I continue to see, even as a grown man, the deep need in my own life for limits, rhythms, and boundaries. I want to rule my spirit and these things help.

THE GOAL OF SELF-CONTROL: ETERNAL LIFE

Paul discusses his need to control himself in the context of eternal realities. "Every athlete exercises self-control in all things. They do it to receive a perishable wreath, but we an imperishable" (1 Cor 9:25). We are seeking an eternal prize that cannot be taken from us. The glory that awaits us motivates us to discipline ourselves now.

He also understands that there is a link between his self-control and receiving this eternal life: "But I discipline my body and keep it under control, lest after preaching to others I myself should be disqualified" (1 Cor 9:27). Read that sentence carefully. Paul is concerned that he will preach the gospel of Jesus to others, helping them to receive eternal life—and then turn around and *be disqualified himself* because he lacks discipline over his own body. What a remarkable tragedy that would be! Paul wants self-control because Paul wants eternal life with God.

In a later letter, he returns to this picture of running a race: "I press on toward the goal for the prize of the upward call of God in Christ Jesus" (Phil 3:14). "Press on" here means to pursue something by running. He runs hard toward the goal because he wants the prize. If we want eternal life, we put forth the effort to receive it.

These connections can lead to some misconceptions. Paul is not saying, "You have to discipline yourself or you can't be saved." Nor is he claiming that only if we work hard enough at self-control will we receive eternal life. The danger here is that *when we are not self-controlled, we will again be sucked into a life of slavery to sin.* If we start to sin, we may end up back where we started, only worse. This is a real danger and it really happens.

Peter speaks of some false teachers troubling his audience:

> They promise them freedom, but they themselves are slaves of corruption. For whatever overcomes a person, to that he is enslaved. For if, after they have escaped the defilements of the world through the knowledge of our LORD and Savior Jesus Christ, they are again entangled in them and overcome, the last state has become worse for them than the first (2 Pet 2:19-20).

Notice Peter's wording carefully. These false teachers have "escaped the defilements of the world" by being forgiven of their sins. But now they are "again entangled in them and overcome." He does not refer to an occasional mistake, but a return to sin-slavery. They have become *"slaves of corruption"* again. This is not merely a false teacher problem; it is a human problem. *Self-control is essential because I know firsthand how dangerous sin can be. I can't toy with it. Too much has been done to set me free from sin. I won't, I can't, go back there.*

This perspective gives fuel for self-discipline. Peter urges us to "make every effort to supplement your faith with virtue, and virtue with knowledge, and knowledge with self-control" (2 Pet 1:5-6). Why? "if you practice these qualities you will never fall" (2 Pet 1:10) and "in this way there will be richly provided for you an entrance into the eternal kingdom of our LORD and Savior Jesus Christ" (2 Pet 1:11). We keep adding to our faith because *we keep looking forward*.

This necessitates a paradigm shift—one that should permeate Christian homes. We move from a focus on the temporary to the eternal, from the short-term to the long-term. When a Christian is unwilling to work on self-control, he is "so nearsighted that he is blind, having forgotten that he was cleansed from his former sins" (2 Pet 1:9). Being "nearsighted" is the problem here. It resonates with me because I am nearsighted. Without glasses or contacts, people and objects from about 10 feet away from me and out become blurry beyond recognition. It is very frustrating. I know there is something there, but I can't see it with any clarity. In some settings it is extremely dangerous. *Peter warns us that without self-control, we are blind to our past (forgetting we have been cleansed) and to our future (preparing for God's kingdom).* What we need is a change in our focus.

Self-control is about saying no to some things now in anticipation of a bigger, deeper, ultimate yes. So in our homes, anything that pushes us toward that perspective shift will be worthwhile. We encourage our children to save money, saying no now for yes later. We encourage our children to be patient with other people, giving leniency now for a benefit later. We encourage our children to work hard and study, giving up fun now for fun later. If we save this now, we can have a great vacation. Because young children struggle with abstract concepts like future rewards, it is vital that parents keep talking about what is coming. Then, when the time comes, we can strongly reinforce the lesson.

I would add a caution—from personal experience—about how spouses can sometimes help (and sometimes hurt) each other's self-control efforts. When I am seeking some relief from intense discipline—whether it's a late night run to IHOP, a spending splurge, or a desire to rant out my frustrations about a person—my wife is the first person I involve. Because we love our mates, we might be tempted to enable their lack of discipline. We can be each other's enabler or helper. Gentle pushback from such an important source can help turn the tide.

Honey is good and having company is fun. Can we tell ourselves no? Home is a place where we identify our self-control struggles and begin to work to improve them. It is a place where we embrace the beauty of living under control in submission to Jesus. It is a place where children grow to tell themselves no and prepare for a better future.

We control ourselves.

For Personal Introspection

- In what areas of my life do I struggle with self-control? Does my family know about this? What am I doing to work on this?
- Do I feel that I have been set free from slavery to sin? What has that looked like in my life?
- Am I focused on the short-term or long-term? How do I know?

For Discussion

- Is self-control natural? Why do some people seem to be more in control of themselves than others?
- The author claims that "self-control is the way to true freedom." Do you agree? How is this true? Why would some dispute that claim?
- Why are limits important for kids? For adults?
- How do we embrace rhythms? Why does this matter?
- Explain the relationship between self-control and eternal life.

RULE

10

Just Because You're Angry Doesn't Mean You're Right

From the very first family, we learn what anger can do in the home. When Jehovah accepts Abel's offering but rejects his brother Cain's, Cain is "very angry and his face fell" (Gen 4:5). The anger festers and grows. "Cain spoke to Abel his brother. And when they were in the field, Cain rose up against his brother Abel and killed him" (Gen 4:8). Cain destroys his brother, his family, and his life because he acts out of his anger.

We have a modern name for this age-old problem: domestic violence. Domestic violence statistics are chilling. In America, 1 in 3 women and 1 in 4 men have experienced some form of physical violence by an intimate partner. 1 in 4 women and 1 in 7 men have been victims of severe physical violence (such as beating, burning, or strangling).[1] 72% of all murder-suicides involve an intimate partner, and 94% of the victims of murder-suicides are female.[2] Horrific as they are, statistics only tell part of the story: every year, millions of terrifying encounters, millions of fresh emotional wounds given to

---

1. https://www.cdc.gov/violenceprevention/pdf/nisvs_report2010-a.pdf
2. https://www.vpc.org/studies/amroul2012.pdf

cowering children, millions of homes torn apart. *Christian homes simply must be different.*

We have looked at length about the need to make home a safe space. But the danger is that we assume that such statistics—and horrible stories like Cain's—are the result of evil psychopaths. We must see that such problems are almost always a result of not controlling our anger. *And we all struggle with controlling our anger.* It is our anger that leads us to yell and argue and throw things. It is our anger that leads to words that permanently scar our mates and children. And it is anger that occasionally leads to outright violence.

Even more shocking is that when God confronts Cain about what he has done, *he is defiant*. When God asks him where Abel is, he mouths off: "I do not know; am I my brother's keeper?" (Gen 4:9). When God calls him out for murder and sentences him to wander the earth, Cain complains about that: "My punishment is greater than I can bear" (Gen 4:13). There is no remorse, no confession, no acknowledgement of sin. Cain is unrepentant because *he is convinced that he is right to be angry*. Anger clouds our judgment and keeps us from seeing how we are acting and whether it is justified.

Just because you're angry doesn't mean you're right.

ANGER IS OFTEN MISINFORMED AND MISDIRECTED

This sad story begins when both brothers bring an offering to God. Abel, the shepherd, brings one of the firstborn of his flock. Cain, a farmer, brings some of his crops. "And the LORD had regard for Abel and his offering, but for Cain and his offering he had no regard. So Cain was very angry, and his face fell" (Gen 4:4-5). We are not told why God has no respect for Cain's offering. But I love the fact that God does not just leave Cain stewing in his anger. Like the older brother in Jesus' prodigal son story (Luke 15:28), God goes out to reason with his angry and resentful child. "The LORD said to Cain, 'Why are you angry, and why has your face fallen? If you do well, will you not be accepted? And if you do not do well, sin is crouching at the door. Its desire is for you, but you must rule over it'" (Gen 4:6-7). God questions Cain: why are you angry? God reassures Cain: if you do well, you will be accepted! The problem is not God or Abel, but that "sin is crouching at the door." Cain is in danger and needs to pay attention. Unresponsive to God's warning, Cain lets his anger simmer until it boils over in violence.

It is not that Cain should never get angry. It would be understandable if Cain is angry *with himself* for not making a proper sacrifice. It would be understandable if Cain is angry *with God* for not accepting his sacrifice. He wouldn't be right, but we could understand it. What doesn't make sense is that Cain would be angry at *Abel*, who has done nothing except try to please God. Cain's anger is misinformed and misdirected.

When Joseph's brothers sell him into Egyptian slavery, he serves in Potiphar's house. Jehovah blesses Joseph's work there, but he soon catches the eye of Potiphar's wife. He repeatedly spurns her advances, so she lies about it and makes false accusations against Joseph.

> Then she laid up his garment by her until his master came home, and she told him the same story, saying, 'The Hebrew servant, whom you have brought among us, came in to me to laugh at me. But as soon as I lifted up my voice and cried, he left his garment beside me and fled out of the house.' As soon as his master heard the words that his wife spoke to him, 'This is the way your servant treated me,' his anger was kindled. And Joseph's master took him and put him into the prison, the place where the king's prisoners were confined (Gen 39:16-20).

Of course Potiphar is angry when he hears this. Who wouldn't be? It is not anger that is the problem here; it is that his anger is *misinformed*. And because it is misinformed, it becomes misdirected. Joseph suffers unfairly.

I have had this experience with my kids. One of them comes to me and says, "he hit me in the face." I'm angry. I don't want one of my kids to hurt another. I march into the room, ready to dispense justice and give a piece of my mind. But when I hear the full story, I learn more. They were wrestling and the hitting was inadvertent—or something flew across the room and accidentally struck the other—or the other one hit him first. *Suddenly my anger is changed because the information is changed. Sometimes I even get angry with the other one!* This is the nature of anger. We can feel it without being certain of our information or the object of our anger. *Just because you're angry doesn't mean you're right.*

We have already looked at the story Nathan tells King David after his sin with Bathsheba. He describes a rich man who takes a poor man's one ewe lamb. David's reaction to the story is important: "Then David's anger was greatly kindled against the man, and he said to Nathan, 'As the LORD lives, the man who has done this deserves to die, and he shall restore the lamb fourfold, because he did this thing, and because he had no pity" (2 Sam 12:5-6). David's anger is justified; this is a gross injustice. The issue is not that David's anger is misinformed, but that it is *misdirected*. He does not realize that *he is the miscreant*. David himself is the one who deserves to die. In condemning another, he condemns himself.

All of these stories teach us something about anger. They remind us that anger is often a hair-trigger response. Maybe we feel shamed and lash out, like Cain. Maybe we hear a report, believe it instantly, and act rashly, like Potiphar. Maybe we judge quickly and don't realize that we are judging ourselves, like David. But in each situation, there is something wrong with their anger. Our anger is not right simply because it *feels* right. We might have the wrong information or direct our anger at the wrong person. Just because you're angry doesn't mean you're right.

Have you ever had someone speak harshly to you when you had done nothing to them? Sometimes people have been angry with me because of what they *think* I'm saying, even if it's not what I mean. Sometimes their reaction is so disproportionate that it is clear it has nothing to do with me at all. It has helped me to realize that they are not really angry with *me*. They are hurt and angry about a situation in the past and now they're taking it out on me. Anger can be misdirected.

Have you ever had stress at work—frustrated with your boss, for example—and then gotten angry with your family? We feel helpless to tell our boss how we really feel, so we bring the hostility home and force it on people who *have* to listen to us. Anger can be misdirected.

In situations like these, we don't need to be told to quit being angry. The anger may be justified. What we need is *the space to admit that our anger may be misinformed or misdirected*. Christian homes should be places where instead of merely acting out of our anger, we are free to question our anger. We refuse to blindly assume we are right simply because we feel right. We seek to find out all the facts. We are careful not to take out anger on those who do not deserve it. We interrupt the cycle of anger and think seriously about why we are feeling the way we are. We live the rule: *just because you're angry doesn't mean you're right*.

ANGER OFTEN CLOUDS OUR JUDGMENT

God attempts to reason with Cain. "Sin is crouching at the door." "Why are you angry, and why has your face fallen?" These are the words of a concerned friend. Cain won't listen. He is angry and he feels right in his anger. So he kills his brother. He seeks a permanent solution to a temporary problem. It is tragically poor judgment. Then he feels so justified that he barks back at God when confronted. Cain is just so convinced that he is right that all actions or words are appropriate. He cannot see himself objectively anymore. He would kill his brother a thousand more times. He was right to kill him. This kind of clouded judgment is what anger does.

In this way, anger is a lot like alcohol. One of the dangers of alcohol is that it lowers our inhibitions and we begin to consider doing and saying things that we never would if sober. When we are in the moment—under the influence—what we are doing feels right and appropriate. But for those outside, it seems unbelievable. This is what anger does.

Nebuchadnezzar, the king of Babylon, is the most powerful man on earth. Yet when he is defied by three Jewish men, he loses it. "Then Nebuchadnezzar was filled with fury, and the expression of his face was changed against Shadrach, Meshach, and Abednego. He ordered the furnace heated seven times more than it was usually heated" (Dan 3:19). He was mad before; now he is furious. We can picture him—a great, finely-dressed king, purple with rage. The veins in his forehead are bulging. His eyes get big. He snarls and grits his teeth. And he does some very foolish things. He orders his servants to heat the furnace seven times hotter than normal, which will kill some of his mighty men. What sense does this make? At any temperature, the furnace will kill Shadrach, Meshach, and Abednego. Will he kill them deader than dead? He is too mad to think straight. This is what anger does.

Jonah is angry because God has saved the people of Nineveh, whom he feels should be destroyed. Now Jonah has become God's instrument to *save* them. It doesn't sit well with him. "But it displeased Jonah exceedingly, and he was angry...And the LORD said, 'Do you do well to be angry?'" (Jonah 4:1, 4). Just as he does with Cain, God challenges Jonah's anger. Are you right about this? Jonah insists that he is right to be angry, just as defiant as Cain (Jonah 4:9). Jonah looks at God's mercy as a weakness (Jonah 4:2). In his finer moments, I suspect that Jonah would know better than to be this belligerent and ugly toward God. But when we're angry, we act differently. We make foolish decisions. We say dumb things. We are just so, so convinced that we are right. "Yes, I do well to be angry, angry enough to die" (Jonah 4:9).

My suspicion is that I don't need extensive scripture to prove this. What's the dumbest thing *you've* done while angry? We all have some stories. Most of us associate those things with great shame. We are embarrassed and wonder what we were thinking. I have witnessed people kicking dents in cars, threatening others with guns, and smashing expensive electronics. I have injured myself in my anger. I have yelled at people and thrown things at them. I have smashed a window. In every case, given a moment of calm, I would not have done those things. What about you?

And the real danger is that *when we're angry, we don't even seem to notice that our reasoning is impaired.* Like Jonah, we need to remember that *just because we're angry doesn't mean we're right.*

Christian homes must be places where we *acknowledge that decisions made in anger are often unwise, ungodly, and dangerous.* Parents of younger children have this opportunity when our kids have a negative interaction with another child. When they are unfairly treated, our instinct is to rush to their defense in our anger, protecting them. In such situations, parents must model a blend of supporting our children while not lashing out because we are upset. Can we talk through such things calmly and kindly? Can we show support without badmouthing the other child? Can we counsel our children the best way to handle emotional situations? If our children are looking to us as models of how to live with anger, what are we teaching them?

Christian homes also must rely on the principle that *differences are better resolved by reasoning than by pure emotion.* We will get angry with each other from time to time. Spouses will disagree. Siblings will annoy one another. It is when we value reasoning that we introduce the possibility that *I may be wrong to be angry.* "Tell me why you're angry." "What are you feeling?" "What do you think is the best solution for both of us?". These phrases change the tenor of our homes, promoting collaborative conversation in place of angry outburst. *Just because you're angry doesn't mean you're right.*

ANGER OFTEN DOES DAMAGE

Cain will forever remember this day. He is separated from his parents and his life as a farmer. He is a vagabond from now on. Adam and Eve will forever remember this day. It is a day of unspeakable tragedy for everyone. And it is all the result of Cain's anger.

I wonder how many people there are in our world who have a dark day like this in their history. A day when the story of their lives turned. A day when they got so angry that they did something they could never reverse. And when the anger cooled and they saw themselves in the cold light of day, they became consumed with regret.

Anger does damage. Domestic violence does not happen merely because people are psychopaths. It happens because ordinary people get angry at the people they love most and know best—and do things they forever regret. Christian homes should *never, never* be places where physical violence or abuse are tolerated.

The damage is not just physical. It is terrifying when someone is truly angry. The terror is not specific; it is the shocking realization that someone is out of control and we have no idea what they will do. The prospect is horrible, especially for a child. That cowering fear—that terror that now you need protection from the people who are supposed to protect you—does damage.

But the most common kind of damage anger does is the emotional devastation that comes from awful words said to us. We have spoken extensively about the power and importance of speech in our homes. But why do we say such things to those we love? Why do we wound and lash out verbally? Anger. What is really damaging about anger expressed in words is that *we are afraid that angry people are finally telling us the truth.* When someone tells me I'm lazy, I'm greedy, I'm ugly, I'm stupid, I'm selfish, or I'm a loser, I'm worried that's what they really think. They are finally being honest. That hurts. We are wounded.

I am convinced that all people need a deeper awareness of the damage *our* anger can do, especially in the home. There is a reason that Jesus tells us that to deal with murder, we need to work on anger (Matt 5:21-22). There is a reason Paul tells us to be angry and *do not sin* (Eph 4:26). There is a reason that anger is listed in the works of the flesh (Gal 5:20). *It damages other people.*

As I prepared these thoughts and studied these passages, I went with two of my kids to the lake. I had bought them a special frisbee for around $10. As we drove to the lake, I stressed to them to be careful with the frisbee, to take care of it, and to be sure not to throw it into the lake. I said this several times. You can guess what happened. The frisbee went in the lake. They told me when we got in the car to leave the lake. I was furious. I had told them so many times! They were just being so careless and wasteful. I slammed my phone on the console. I raised my voice. I ranted for a few minutes. Then I looked in the rearview mirror—into my precious child's eyes—and I saw them fill with tears. Not because he had done anything wrong, but because I was so angry. I scared him. Over a $10 piece of plastic. Immediately, my heart broke. I apologized to him. I told him that it is OK for me to be frustrated, but I shouldn't have acted like that. But now I have scarred my child's heart—the child that I prayed for and nurtured and loved on and would do anything for. I did that. Anger does damage.

For every little girl who has cowered in the corner or cried in the closet, waiting for Mom and Dad to stop fighting—for every child who has flinched at his father's angry approach—for everyone who has just escaped the house to avoid the excessive wrath of their parents, we owe it to our own family to challenge and control our own anger.

Anger does damage. Even when I'm angry, it doesn't mean I'm right.

JAMES' GUIDE TO HANDLING ANGER

How can we properly deal with anger in our homes? James' three steps fit each of the anger issues we have discussed. "Know this, my beloved brothers: let every person be quick to hear, slow to speak, slow to anger; for the anger of man does not produce the righteousness of God" (James 1:19-20).

Be Quick to Hear

If anger is often misinformed and misdirected, then being quick to hear will help us. The idea here is to *let information, not emotions, drive our decisions*. So Christian homes will emphasize collecting all the information. We are eager to hear as much as we can *before* we respond or decide.

James is not telling us that we should never feel anything lest it influence our decisions inappropriately. He is reminding us that *often we respond without fully understanding the situation*. This is a recipe for disaster. The old cliché "don't shoot the messenger" implies that occasionally we will lash out at a person who is completely uninvolved or merely reporting. Because we feel anger, we don't bother making sure it is properly directed. If I need to be angry, am I sure it is this person I should be angry with?

The book of Joshua tells a story of the time just after Israel conquers the land of Canaan. Two and a half tribes settle on the eastern side of the Jordan, separated from the rest by the river. They build an impressive altar. "And when the people of Israel heard of it, the whole assembly of the people of Israel gathered at Shiloh to make war against them" (Josh 22:12). As soon as they hear of the altar, the other tribes prepare for war. Only when they send a delegation to the other tribes do they understand the situation. The altar is not intended for sacrifices (replacing the proper tabernacle in Shiloh), but as a reminder to all the tribes that they are one people even though separated by the river. Everyone realizes that there is no conflict and war is averted. The amazing thing about this story is that *they are ready to fight before they know whether there is a problem.* Their zeal for maintaining purity in Israel is wonderful; it is their willingness to investigate the situation that seems lacking.

In Deuteronomy, Moses warns of a time when a report of idolatry circulates in Israel. They are not merely to believe such news, but "you shall inquire and make search and ask diligently" (Deut 13:14, see also Deut 17:4). An investigation needs to take place. Ask around. Gather information. Make sure. Be quick to hear.

Am I sure this is accurate? Have I understood the facts? Am I sure that I heard that correctly? Is this what they mean? Christian homes should be places where we learn to *listen.*

Sometimes the words don't come out like we intend them to. Some things sound worse than we intend. Rather than blowing up at each other, we can ask for clarification. Did you mean that? Are you saying ____? We are not in reaction mode, but in information-gathering mode. *Be quick to hear.*

Often poor communication in the home stems from a lack of listening. All members of the family need to be heard—even the quiet ones and small ones. We can ask for each other's opinions. We can listen—deeply listen—to the desires, frustrations, and needs of our spouses and little ones. Some of the things we hear may frustrate or anger us, but our homes will be blessed by being quicker to listen than to react.

In their early days of schooling, my kids would come home with lots to say about their fellow classmates. They would tell of other students who were out of control in class, or who said ugly things to them, or who were too aggressive on the playground. The more questions I asked, the more information would come out: sometimes *my* kids were also a little loud or out of control—or the other child was troubled, had a learning disability, or a rough childhood—or the offense was a small thing. The tone of Christian homes should be one of reserving judgment, listening carefully, and only growing angry when we are certain it is both justified and properly directed.

Be Slow to Speak

James hits us where we live with this one. One of the reasons anger is such a problem is that we are so quick to let fly with our words. If we really know that anger keeps us from thinking clearly—if we really appreciate the damage that our words can do—*then we really must stop saying the first thing that pops into our heads*. Be slow to speak.

So if anger clouds our judgment, our homes should be places where we *slow down and think our anger through*. Am I right to be angry about this? Is this feeling justified? What about this is bugging me so badly?

Anger is usually symptomatic of deeper issues. When I start to investigate my anger, I find that it is often linked to a perceived lack of respect. I *deserve* to be treated better than this, I think. But do I really? Suddenly I am more introspective than indignant. When I get angry that others are successful or respected or wealthy, a little probing uncovers that I am merely jealous. I feel *I* deserve those things, not them! My anger has alerted me to a character weakness within myself. When I get frustrated with my kids, I find that I am afraid that I am losing control of them. My fear and anxiety, ironically, drive them further from me, increasing my fear and anxiety. Now I am reasoning again—and hopefully growing.

Modeling a "slow to speak" attitude will involve a new strategy for arguing. We do not merely fire back at each other, saying whatever hurtful, angry thing crosses our mind so that we feel better. We are careful with our words. We take time, making sure we are reading the situation accurately and that our words will get us closer to resolution.

Sometimes it means apologizing for angry outbursts by then confessing what is going on in our hearts: I'm sorry I said that. I think I am feeling anxious/jealous/disrespected. My real concern is where this behavior might lead. You shouldn't have done that, but I also shouldn't have responded that way.

Building this practice into a habit may help us hesitate before we say something else we must apologize for.

Be Slow to Anger

If anger does damage, we should be slow to anger. This means that we should not allow ourselves to get angry *too easily or too often*. Christian homes should have a long fuse.

> A man of quick temper acts foolishly (Prov 14:17).

> Whoever is slow to anger has great understanding, but he who has a hasty temper exalts folly (Prov 14:29).

> The vexation of a fool is known at once, but the prudent ignores an insult (Prov 12:16).

> Make no friendship with a man given to anger, nor go with a wrathful man, lest you learn his ways and entangle yourself in a snare (Prov 22:24-25).

The "man of quick temper" has a character issue. Regardless of circumstances, he cannot control himself. He is "given to anger" and "a wrathful man." We all know people whom we have to walk on eggshells around. They are always snapping at others, always opinionated, always upset. *Don't be that person. Be slow to anger.*

In a Christian home, anger should be an "on rare occasions" emotion. When we find ourselves consistently angry, the problem is usually not with overwhelming circumstances. We are making anger into a habit. Inevitably this will spill over into our home dynamics. There should be a place to talk ourselves down from anger, reminding ourselves (and each other) of what is important and what is not.

I would especially encourage us to be aware of the tone in our homes. How regularly do we get seriously angry with each other? Anger can be contagious in this way. "Make no friendship with a man given to anger, nor go with a wrathful man, lest you learn his ways and entangle yourself in a snare" (Prov 22:24-25). The proverbs warn that *being easily angered spreads*.

But isn't the opposite true too? If we learn that we can resolve our differences and live together in harmony *without* habitual anger, *wouldn't we all like that better?* This kind of peace and love is contagious too.

James reminds us that "the anger of man does not produce the righteousness of God" (James 1:20). God does not endorse all our anger, nor is it his will for us to live in continual anger. Be slow to anger.

Cain reminds us that anger has horrible potential for destruction in homes. We know this; we have experienced this; we must remain continually aware of it. Christian homes should be places that are not characterized by anger, but peace, love, and joy.

Just because you're angry doesn't mean you're right.

For Personal Introspection

- How have I experienced others' anger?
- How was anger handled in my home of origin?
- What damage have I done to others in anger?
- What kinds of things make me angry? Why?

For Discussion

- In what situations is it right to be angry?
- What are some ways we can change the tone from emotion to reason in our family decision-making?
- What makes someone a good listener? Why do we struggle so much with listening to each other?
- Explain how someone becomes a person "given to anger." Why does this happen? How can we break that cycle?

Conclusion
Keep Sowing the Seeds!

When in high school, I had a close-knit group of male friends. We were all from a small town and had known each other throughout our school years. We shared interests and perspectives, but we also unwittingly shared something else. At one point it occurred to me that in our core group of five, only one of us lived with both of our parents. The stories and reasons were all different, but all of us dealt with broken homes and had our own issues as a result.

I am heartbroken by the young people I encounter who start life with a series of emotional scars—sexual abuse, habitual neglect, degrading criticism, and emotional unavailability. Yet, tragically, often those same young people grow up to have marriages and children of their own. Damaged and hurting, they are unable to care for their own spouses and kids and inflict a new generation of harm. The cycle continues.

This is not the way God intends life to be.

God intends marriage to be a blessing.

"It is not good that the man should be alone; I will make him a helper fit for him" (Gen 2:18). "Rejoice in the wife of your youth"

(Prov 5:18). Joining two hearts, bodies, and lives together should be good for us. Yet because of the intensity of the emotions involved, our marriages can become the source of nearly unimaginable heartache. Stung by rejection, fearful of pain, or frustrated by neglect, we face the awful choice of being miserable or being alone. This is not God's will.

God intends children to be a blessing.

"Behold, children are a heritage from the LORD, and the fruit of the womb a reward" (Psalm 127:3). Yes, children are often inconvenient, expensive, demanding, and frustrating. We can be bitter at the loss of our freedom, worn down by the process of child-rearing, or devastated at their rejection of our parenting. But this is not God's will.

God can use these relationships to rewire our thinking from focusing on ourselves to serving others. Through family, we learn about humility and love and submission and honesty and forgiveness. Not only am I blessed simply to have a spouse and/or children, I am blessed by them specifically. They know me like no one else does. They sharpen and challenge me. And in the crucible of the home, all of us are being forged into new people—hopefully according to God's will for us.

Christian homes are places where everyone is safe, respectful (and respected), and honest. Love is communicated clearly and frequently. We don't speak evil of others. We know our roles and follow them, taking responsibility for ourselves. We deal with our issues. We serve one another instead of trying to dominate. We build self-control together and we hold our anger in check. This is the way God intends life to be.

I can't change my past—the hurts and disappointments I experienced in my childhood or even my failures in earlier family life. But I can live the gospel in my home now.

AN ACT OF FAITH

Building a Christian home is an act of faith. We are investing in a future we do not yet see. We are confident that the efforts we make to live out the gospel will bear fruit, whether we experience it now or not. We trust that God will be pleased by the sacrifices we make for one another (even if the world doesn't notice) and that the bonds we build will endure the future assaults of Satan.

This faith is behind the famous proverb about children: "Train up a child in the way he should go; even when he is old he will not depart from it" (Prov 22:6). This is a proverb, not a promise; it is generally true but not always so. Our efforts at following Jesus at home—and teaching our kids—are not a guarantee that they will become believers. It is not even a promise that they will always return to the course we raised them in. So what can we take from the proverb? *Teaching our children will have a life-long impact.* The words we say, the example we live before them, and the direction we point them in will make an impression on them that will never leave them. They may reject it or drift away from it, but in some ways they will never fully escape it. "Even when he is old" he will still remember his youthful training.

This is tremendously reassuring. Parents long to know that something they are doing is making a difference. We keep talking, keep correcting, keep loving, and keep praying. Is it working? We wonder—especially in the early years—whether any of it is sticking at all. As our kids approach adolescence, the anxiety only grows. We know by this time that our teaching about tooth-brushing and shoe-tying has sunk in, but we remain uncertain about moral guidance. "Train up a child in the way he should go; even when he is old he will not depart from it." Keep sowing the seeds!

Seed-sowing is a helpful picture for me. The New Testament frequently uses the image of sowing and/or planting seeds (Luke

8:4-8, 1 Cor 3:6-7, 1 Pet 1:23-25, James 1:21) to represent how faith grows. When we sow seeds, we don't watch each one to see how it does. We don't stare at that patch of ground for hours on end. We throw a bunch of seeds, then a bunch more, then a bunch more. And we assume that somehow, somewhere in there, some of the seeds will grow into plants and bear fruit. We are confident in the God who has invested the power in his word to change lives, so we keep teaching his word.

We sow seeds in our homes. We invest in our marriages. We show love to our spouse. We talk kindly, think of others before ourselves, and interrupt our anger. We deal with our problems, not allowing a latent issue to grow. Each act, each word, each hug are seeds we sow. We teach our kids, talking consistently about the things that matter. We tell them about our God and what a joy it is to serve him. We teach them to treat others with respect and humility. We show them the peace that comes from following Jesus. Each day, each lesson, each discipline, each word are seeds we sow.

Keep sowing the seeds! Be confident that God will work with you!

What starts at home changes the world. God is with us. Let's change the world!

Works Cited

Cialdini, Robert. Influence: Science and Practice. Allyn & Bacon, 2001.

Davids, P.H. The First Epistle of Peter. Wm B. Eerdmans, 1990.

Kidner, Derek. Psalms 1-72: An Introduction and Commentary. InterVarsity Press, 1973.

Peterson, Eugene. The Message: The Bible in Contemporary Language. NavPress, 2005.

Thomas, Gary. Sacred Marriage: What If God Designed Marriage to Make Us Holy More than Make Us Happy. Zondervan, 2000.

Vanier, Jean. Community and Growth: Our Pilgrimage Together. Paulist Press, 2003 reprint.

A Note from the Author

Thanks for reading *House Rules*! I would greatly appreciate your feedback on the book. Would you take a moment to review the book on Amazon? Amazon reviews ensure that more people find *House Rules* and also help me know what readers find helpful or problematic about the book. You can review by searching for the book on Amazon's site and scrolling down to the "Write a review" button.

For more information about other titles, visit my website at jacobhudgins.com.

Thanks!
Jacob Hudgins

Made in the USA
Coppell, TX
08 November 2023